Children are Meant to be Seen and Heard

humor and wisdom for honoring children

PuddleDancer PRESS™

Created by Meiji Stewart

Illustrated by David Blaisdell

Children are Meant to be Seen and Heard
© 1996 by Meiji Stewart

ISBN# 0-9647349-2-3

PuddleDancer Press is an imprint of the
Keep Coming Back Company.
Published in Del Mar, California
P.O. Box 1204, Del Mar, California 92014
619-452-1386

1st Printing

Illustration: David Blaisdell, Tucson, Arizona
Cover design: Kahn Design, Encinitas, California
Book design: Endore, Ink., San Diego, California
Printing: Vaughan Printing, Nashville, Tennessee

For:
my daughter Malia Adele
(the puddledancer)
&
my nephews and nieces,
Sebastien, Emilie, Skye, Luke, Jake, Nannette, Cairo and Kamana
&
all the children everywhere,
and all the people who make the world a better place for them.

Thanks to:
David for the wonderful illustrations. I am blessed to be able to
work with him. Thanks also to Roger and Gita for putting it all
together, almost always under deadline (usually yesterday).
Thanks to Jeff for the delightful book covers, and, even more,
for his friendship. Thanks to Julie, Gay, Jane, Regina, Rich and
Zane for making it possible to bring PuddleDancer Press to life.
And thanks to my mom and dad for encouraging me to
pursue my dreams.

Children are likely to live up to
what you believe of them.

Lady Bird Johnson

2

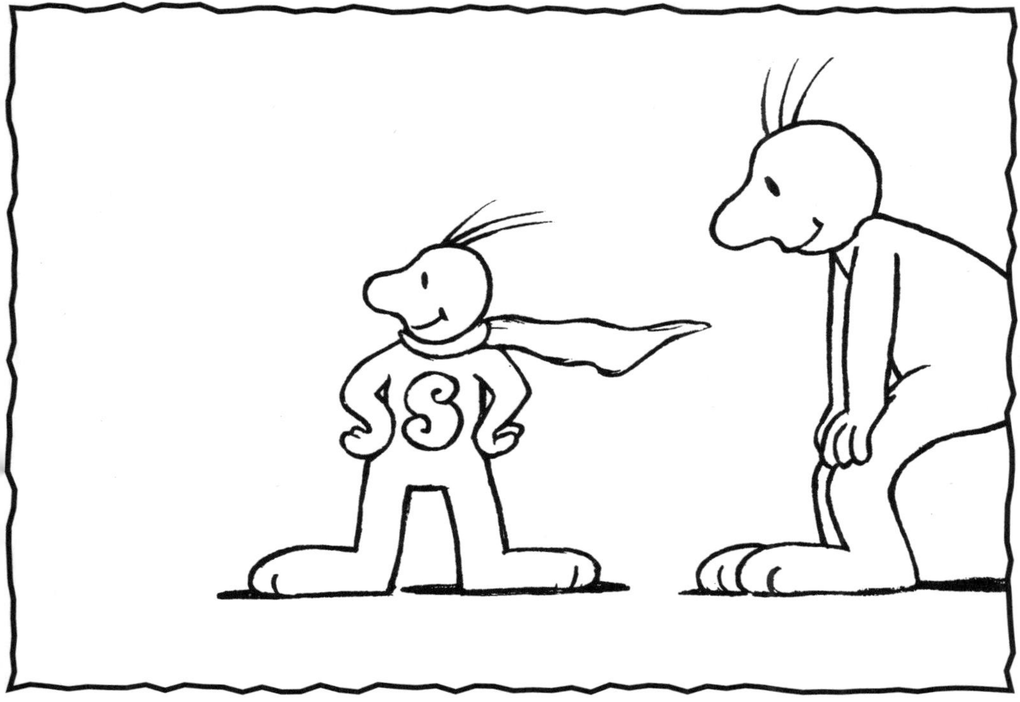

Children reinvent
your world for you.

Susan Sarandon

4

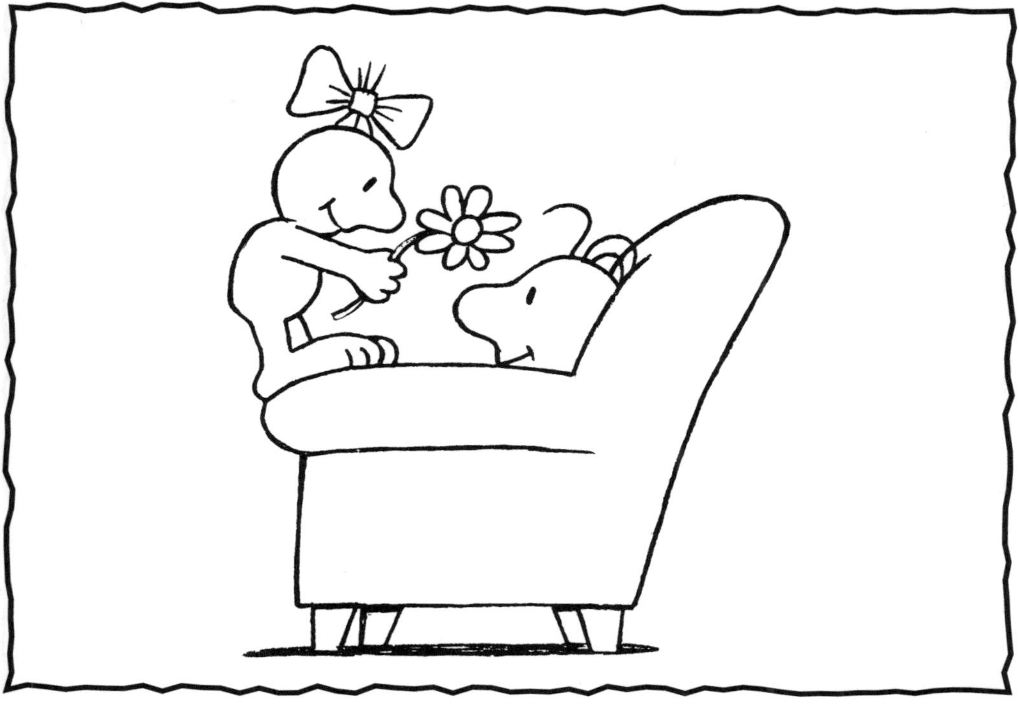

It doesn't hurt your kid's eyesight
to teach them to look on the
bright side of things.

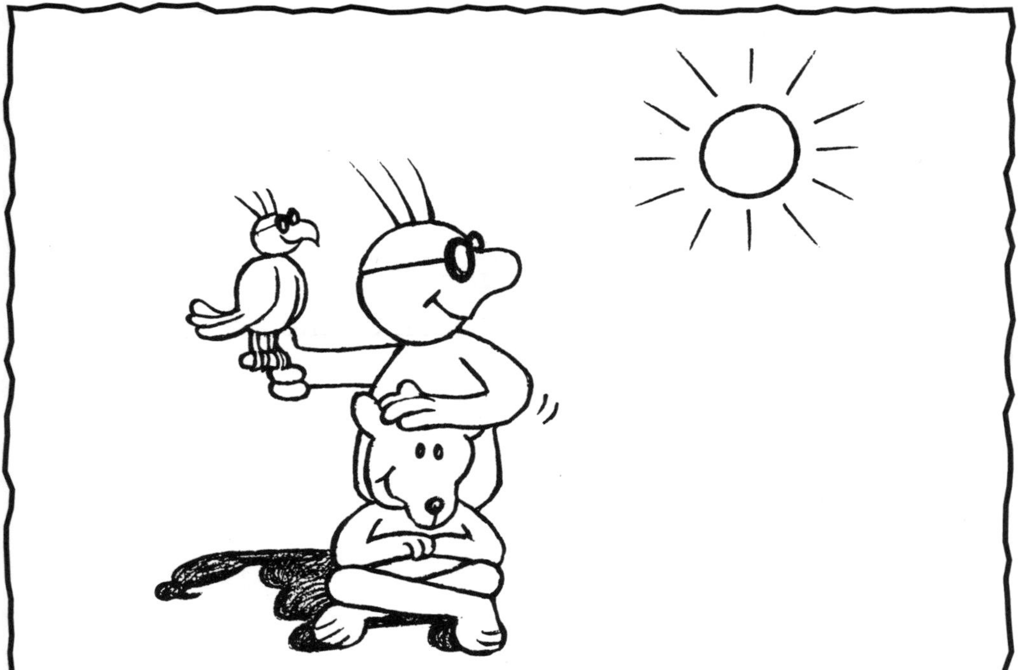

We didn't inherit the land from our fathers;
we are borrowing it from our children.

Amish belief

Parents need to fill a child's bucket
of self-esteem so high that the rest
of the world can't poke enough
holes to drain it up.

Alvin Price

9

I love these little people;
and it is not a slight thing when they,
who are so fresh from God, love us.

Charles Dickens

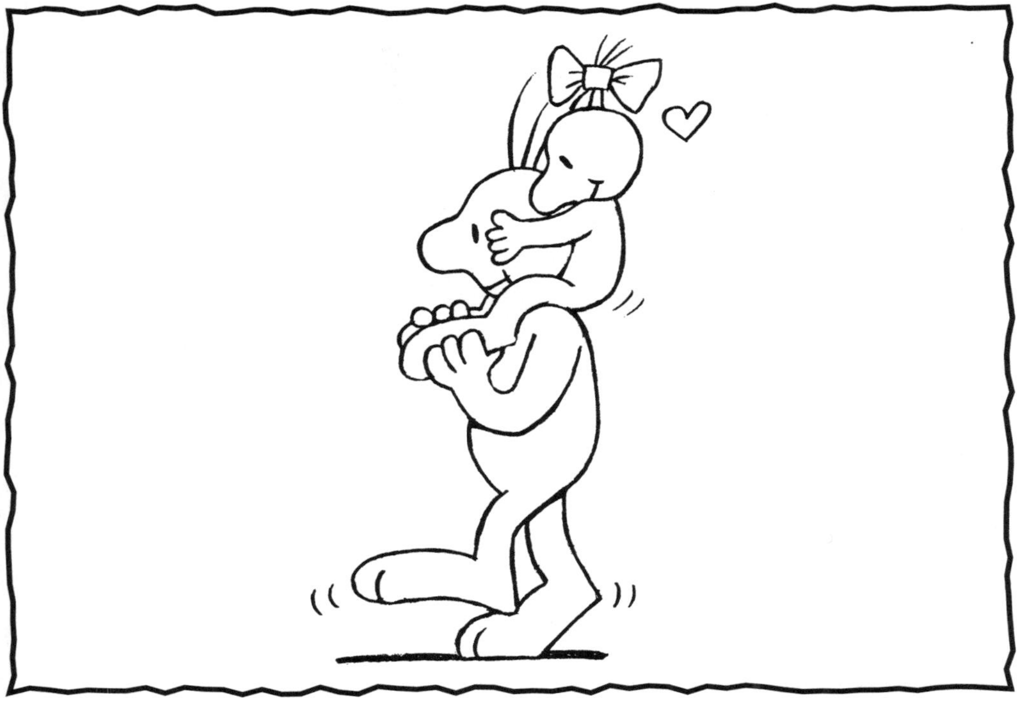

Anyone who thinks
the art of conversation is dead
ought to tell a child
to go to bed.

Robert Gallagher

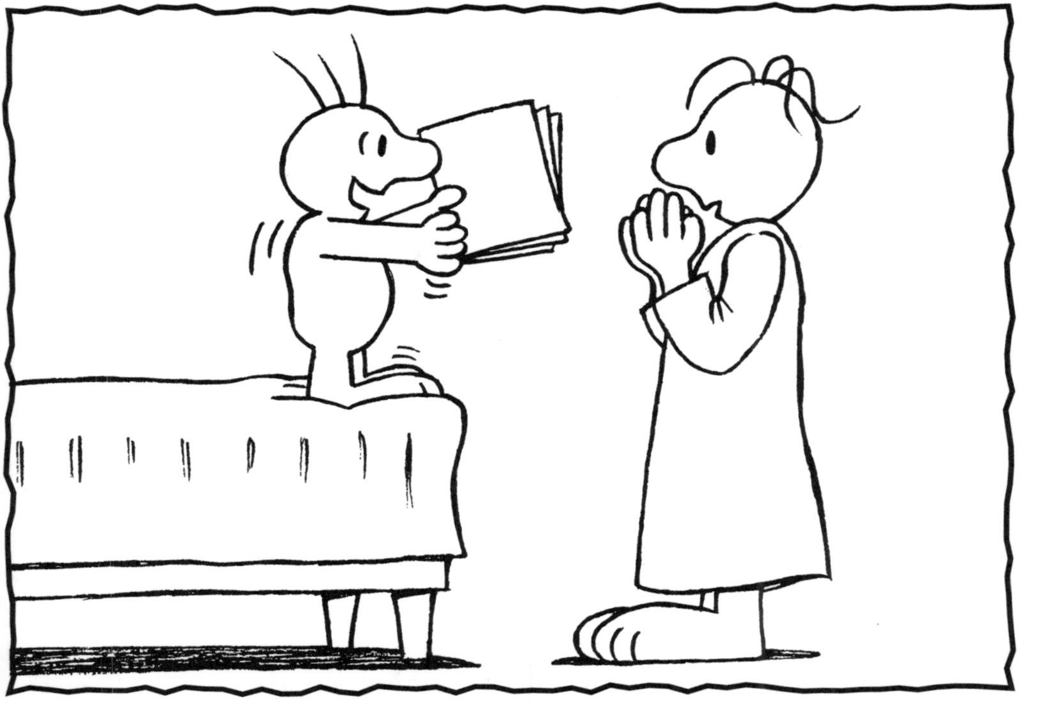

Before I got married I had six theories
about bringing up children; now I have
six children and no theories.

Lord Rochester

Families with babies and families
without babies are sorry for each other.

E.W. Howe

Insanity is hereditary.
You can get it from your children.

Sam Levenson

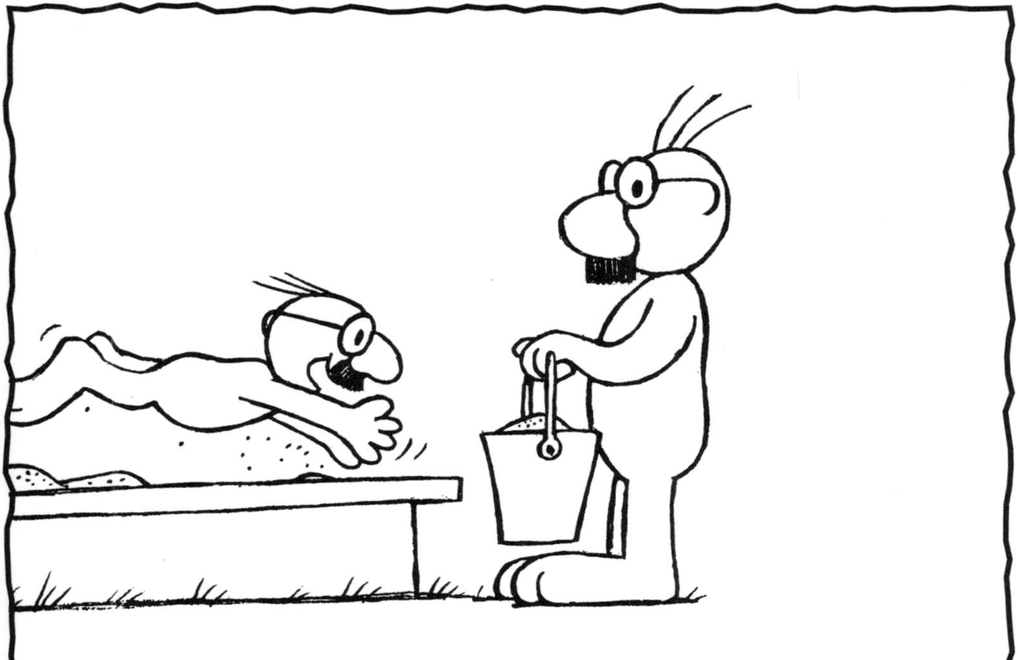

Never help a child with a task
at which he feels he can succeed.

Maria Montessori

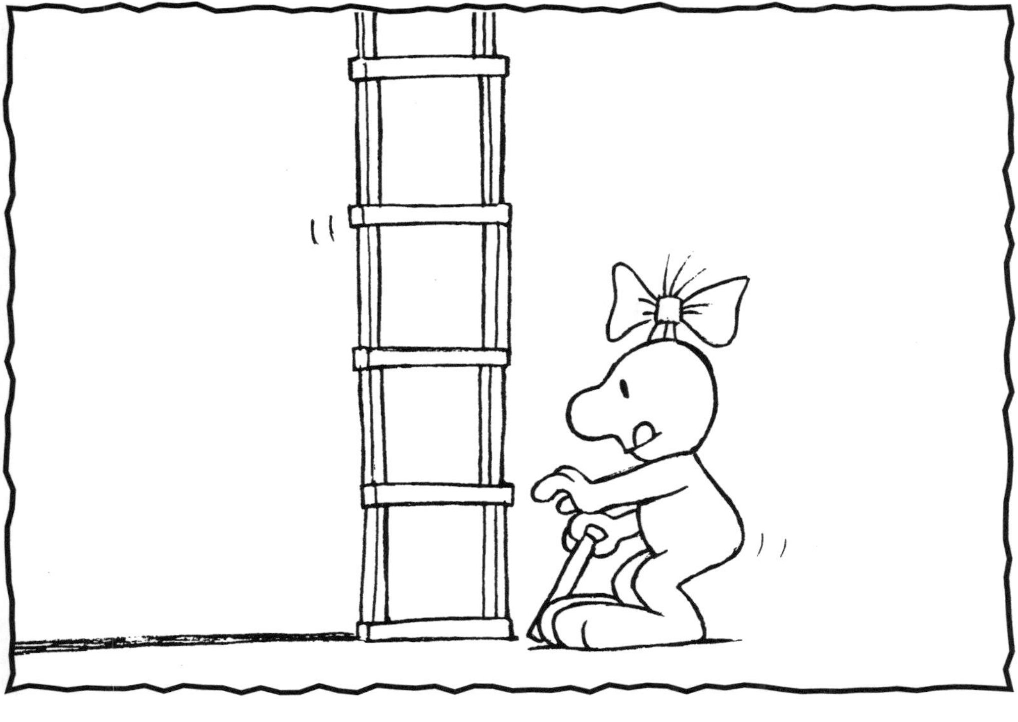

Remember, when they have a tantrum,
don't have one of your own.

Judith Kuriensky

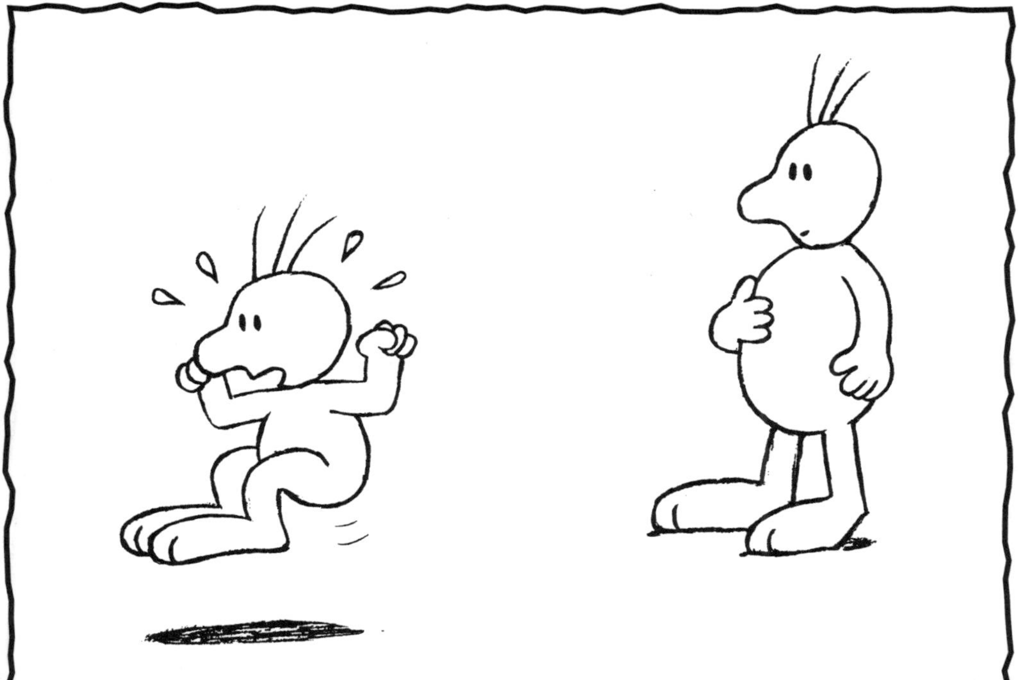

Please think of the children first.
If you ever have anything to do
with their entertainment, their food,
their toys, their custody, their child care,
their health care, their education –
listen to the children,
learn about them,
learn from them.
Think of the children first.

Fred Rogers

People aren't for hitting.
Children are people too.

23

A food is not necessarily essential
just because your child hates it.

Katherine Whiteburn

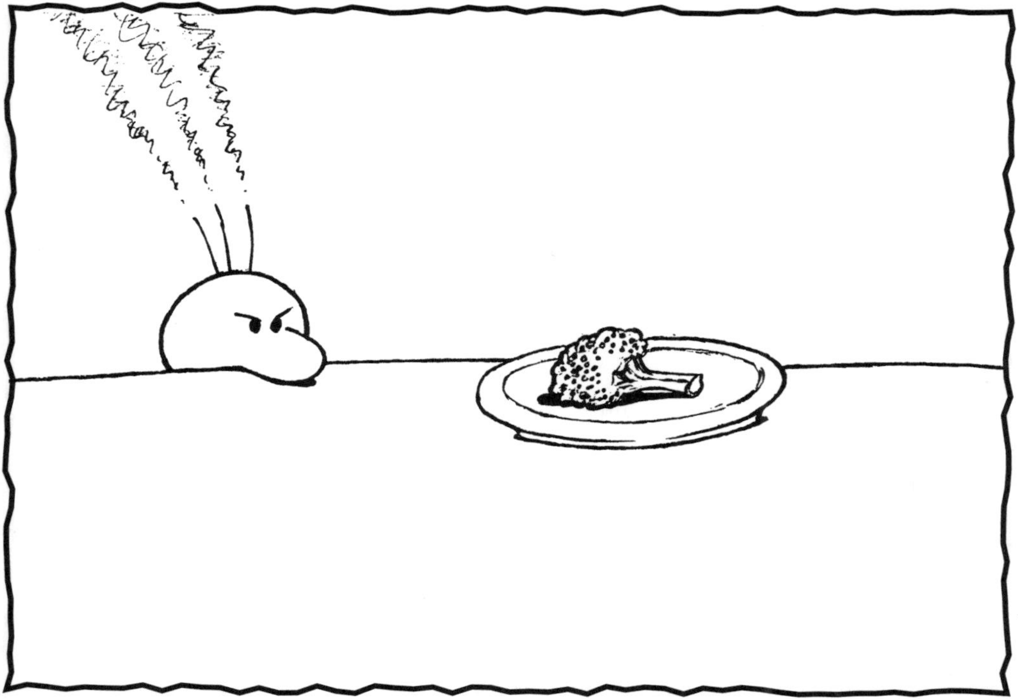

We are all shaped and fashioned
by what we love.

Johann Wolfgang von Goethe

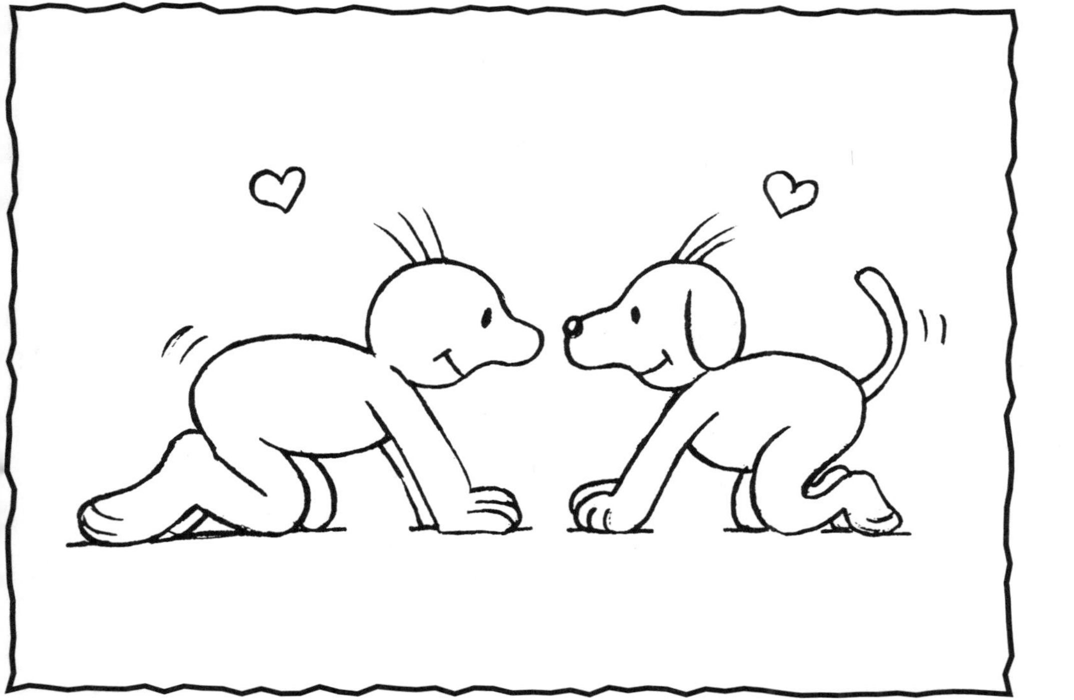

Treat people as if they were what
they ought to be, and you help
them to become what they are
capable of being.

Johann Wolfgang von Goethe

If I could say just one thing to
parents, it would be simply that a
child needs someone who believes
in him no matter what he does.

Alice Keliher

I have often thought
what a melancholy world this would
be without children,
and what an inhuman world,
without the aged.

Coleridge

30

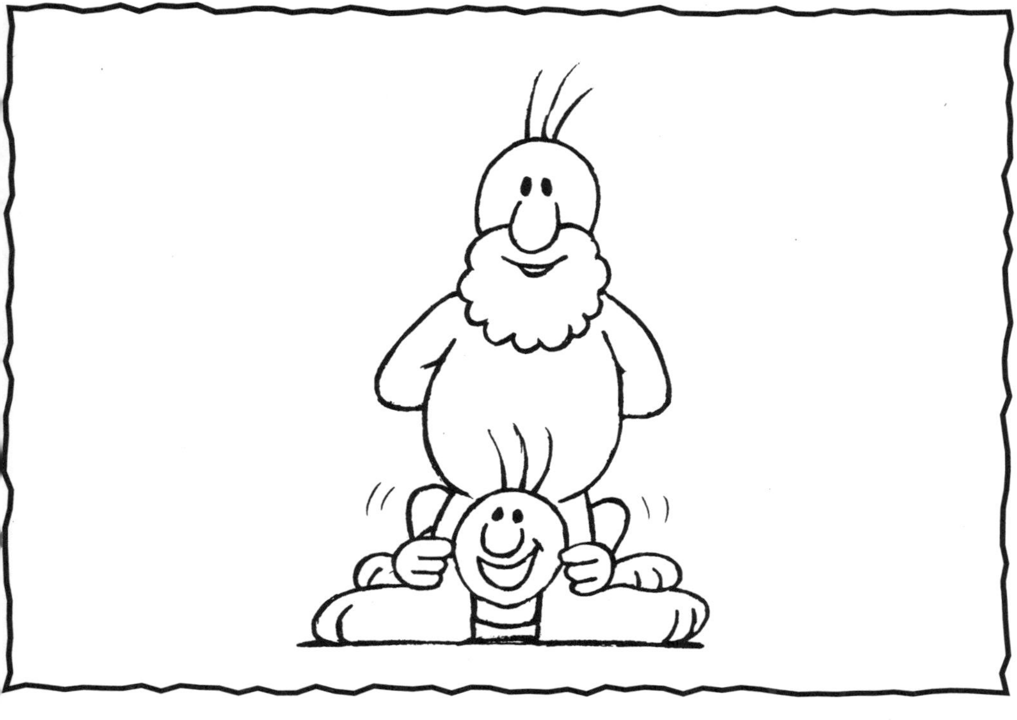

What you do in the present
creates the future,
so use the present to create a
wonderful tomorrow.

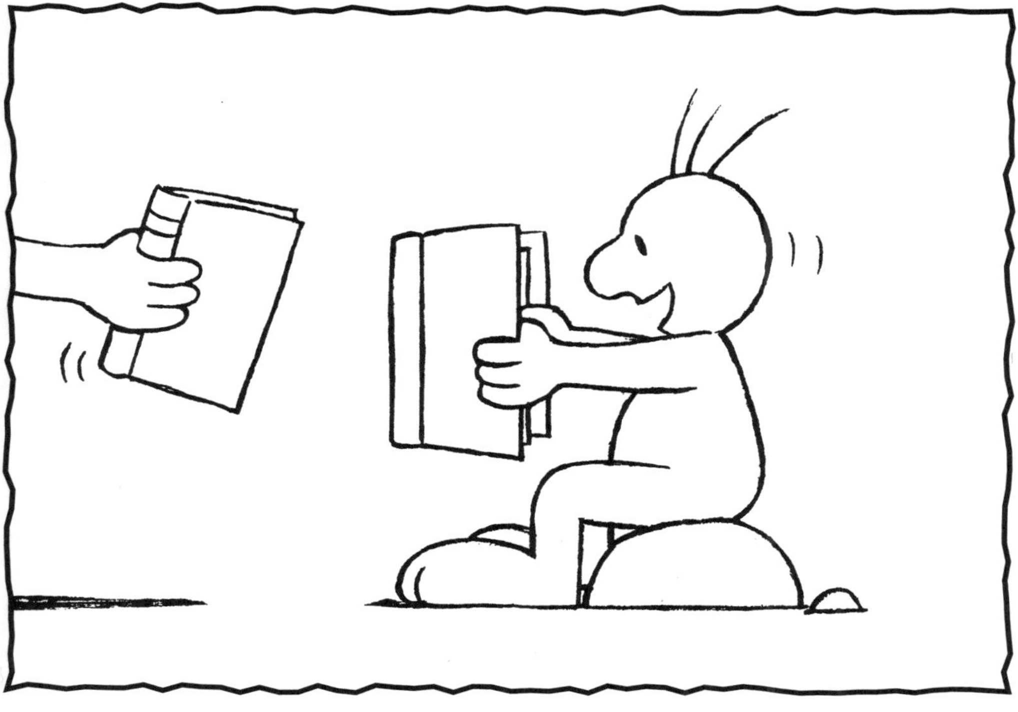

In automobile terms,
the child supplies the power
but the parents have to
do the steering.

Benjamin Spock

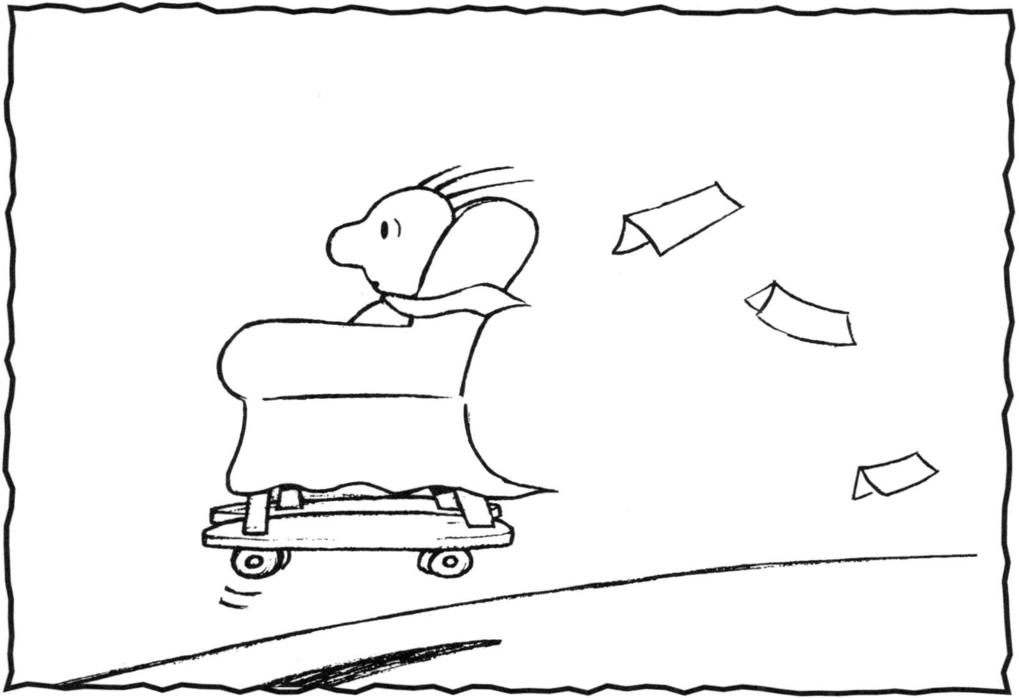

By profession I am a soldier and
take pride in that fact.
But I am prouder, infinitely prouder,
to be a father.

Gen. Douglas MacArthur

36

Never fear spoiling children by
making them too happy.
Happiness is the atmosphere in
which all good affections grow.

Ann Eliza Bray

We speak of educating our children.
Do we know that our children
educate us?

Lydia H. Signouver

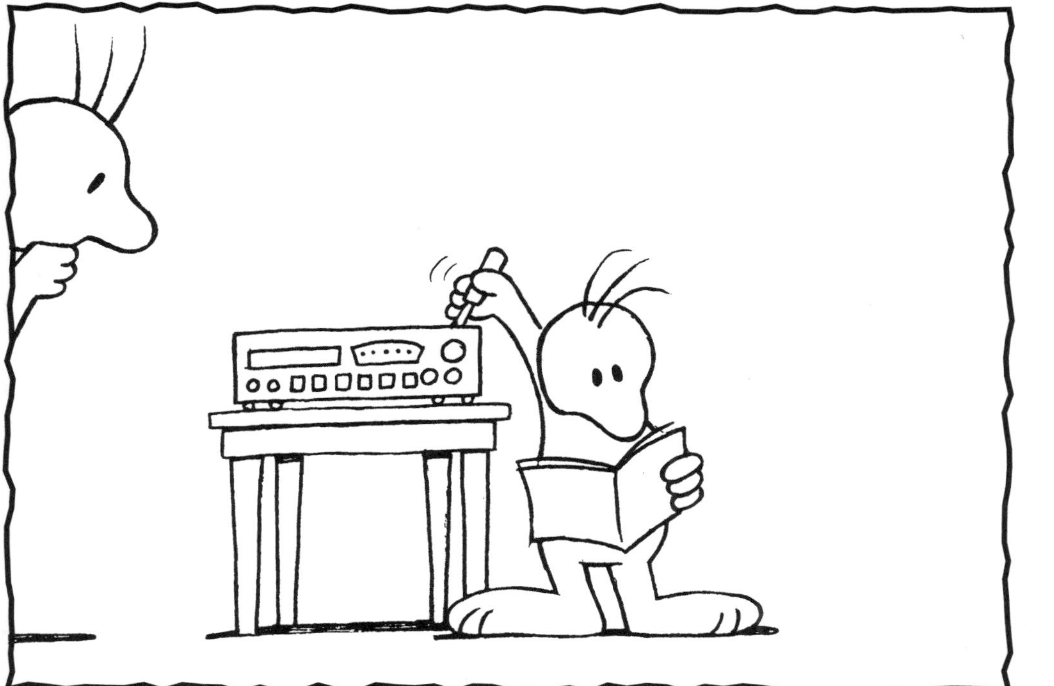

Healthy families remind
each other of their goodness;
unhealthy families remind
each other of their failings.

Matthew Fox

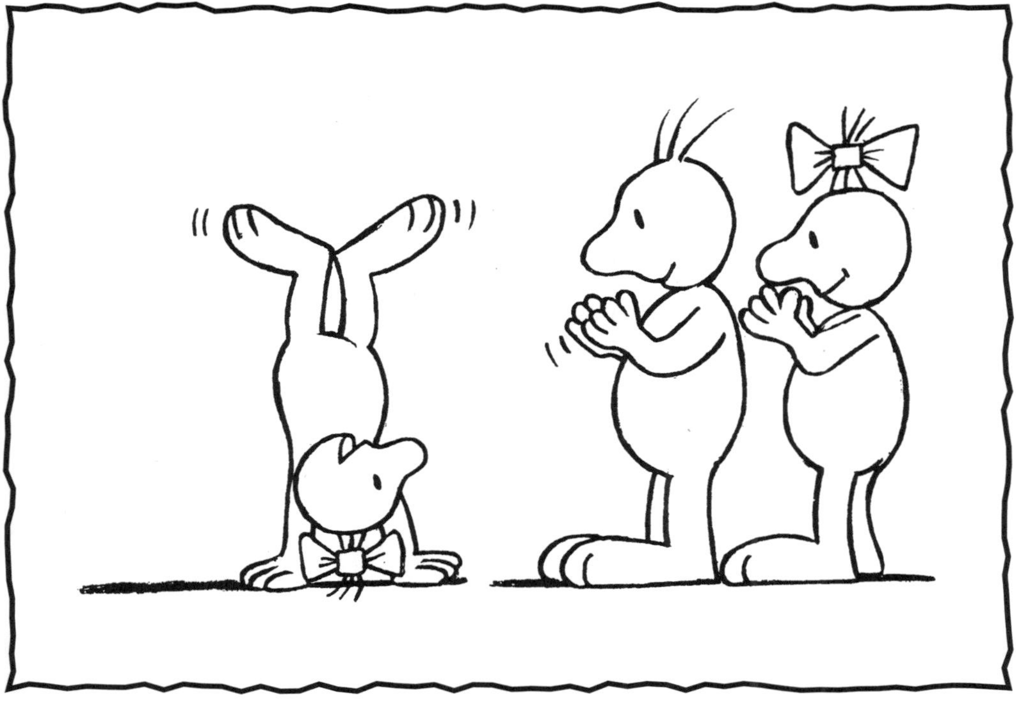

To nourish children and raise them
against odds is, in any time,
any place, more valuable than to
fix bolts in cars or design nuclear weapons.

Marilyn French

Nothing is more important to our shared future than the well-being of children.

Hillary Rodham Clinton

Being a dad is not a spectator sport.

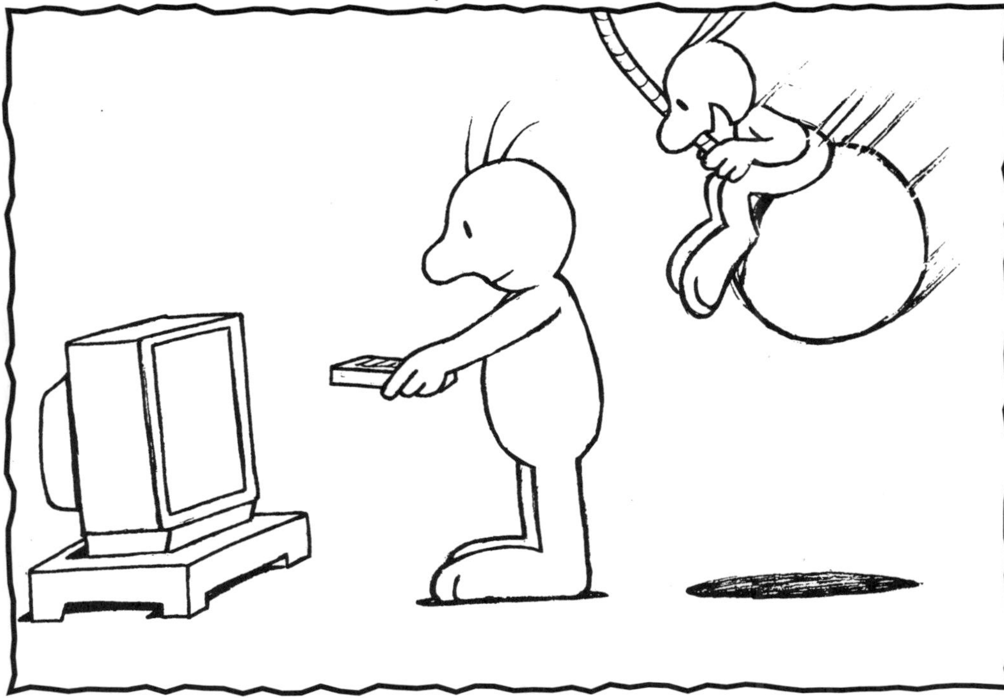

The way to love anything is to realize that it may be lost.

G. K. Chesterton

46

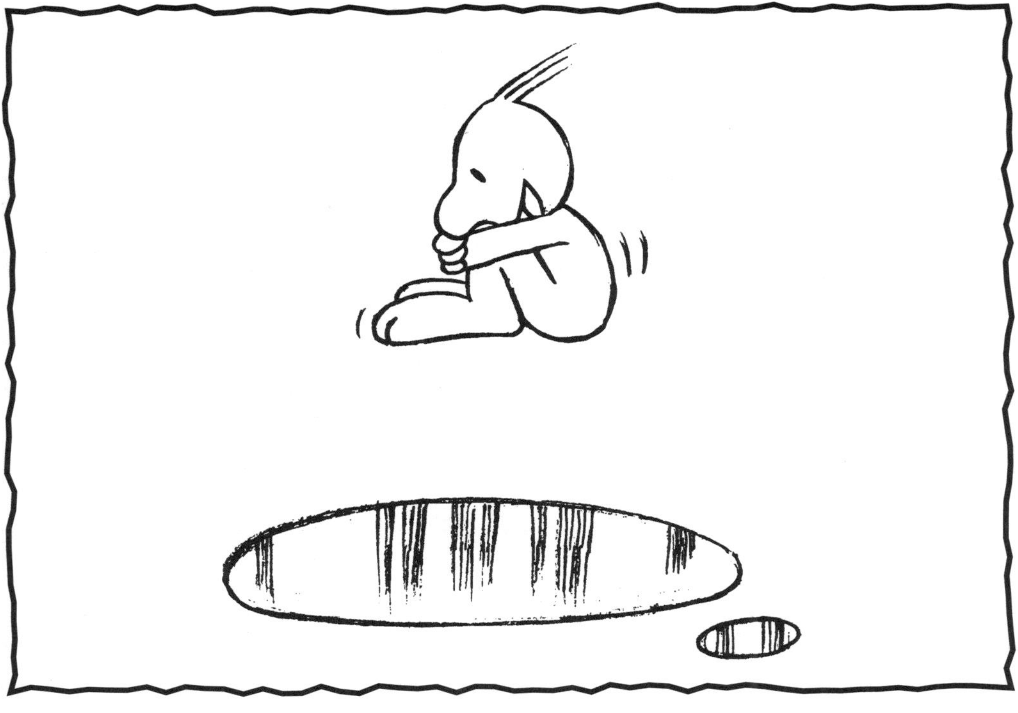

Do you love me because I am beautiful,
or am I beautiful because you love me?

Oscar Hammerstein II

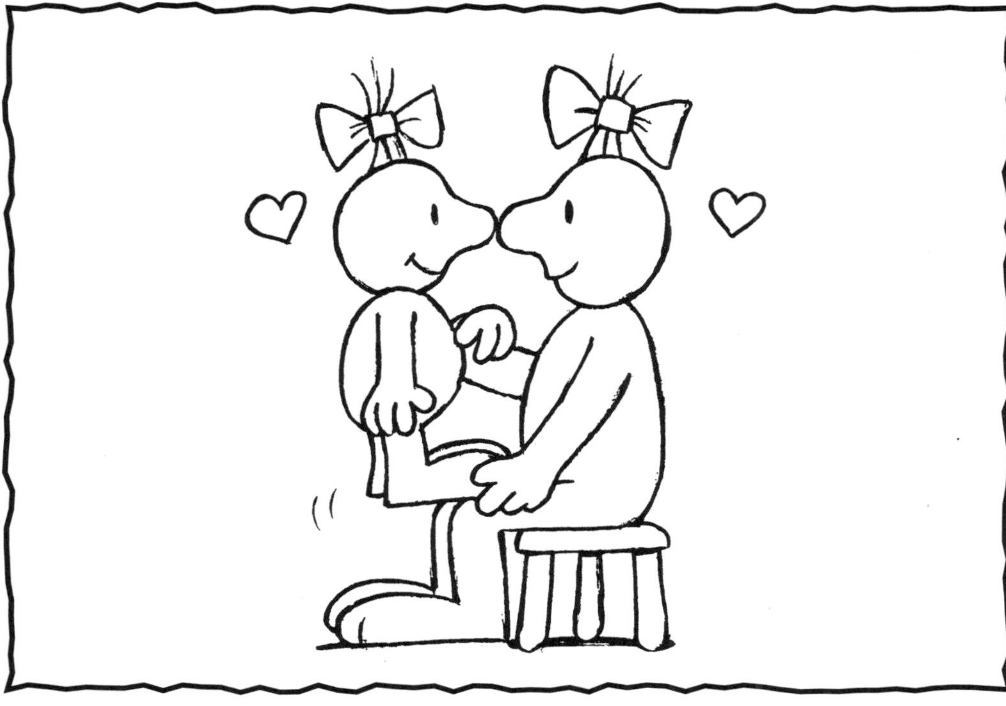

Children spell "LOVE"
..T-I-M-E.

Dr. Anthony P. Witham

Divorces don't wreck children's lives.
People do.

Fred Rogers

A child educated only at school
is not an educated child.

George Santayana

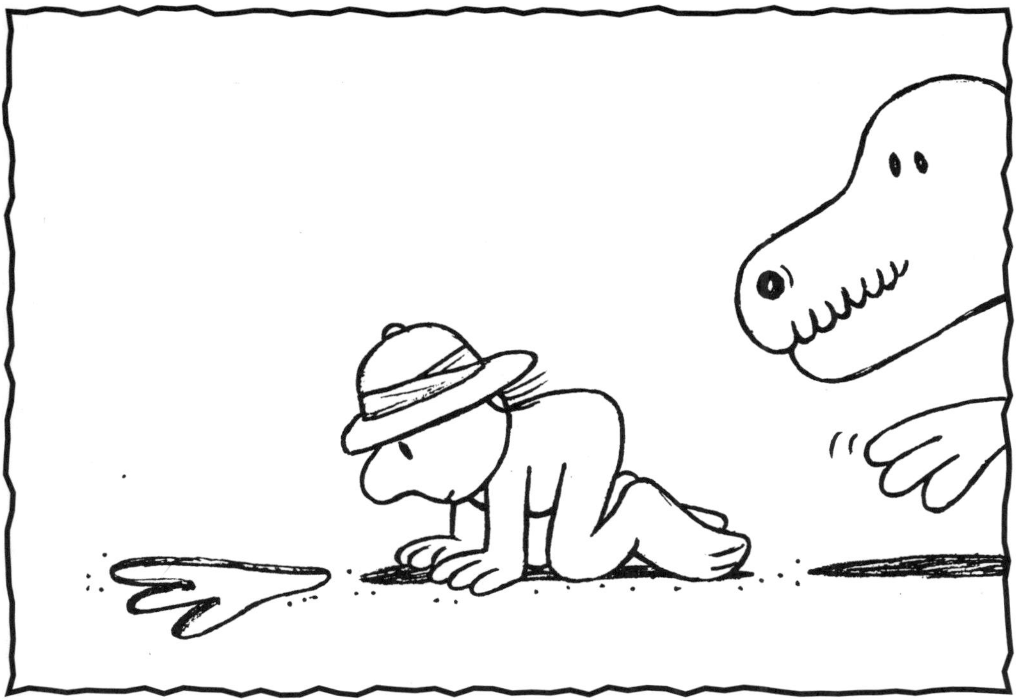

When elephants fight,
it is the grass that suffers.

African saying

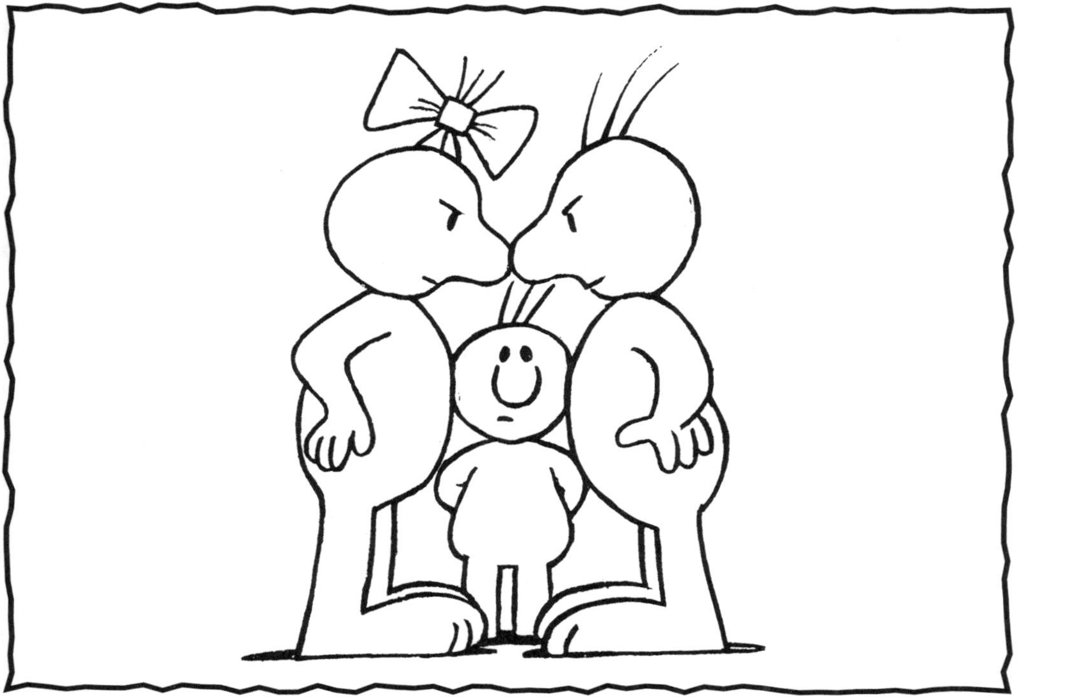

Perhaps once in a hundred years a person may be ruined by excessive praise, but surely once every minute someone dies inside for lack of it.

Cecil G. Osborne

There are only two lasting bequests
we can hope to give our children:
One of these is roots, the other is wings.

Hodding Carter

If you want to be listened to,
you should put in time listening.

Marge Piercy

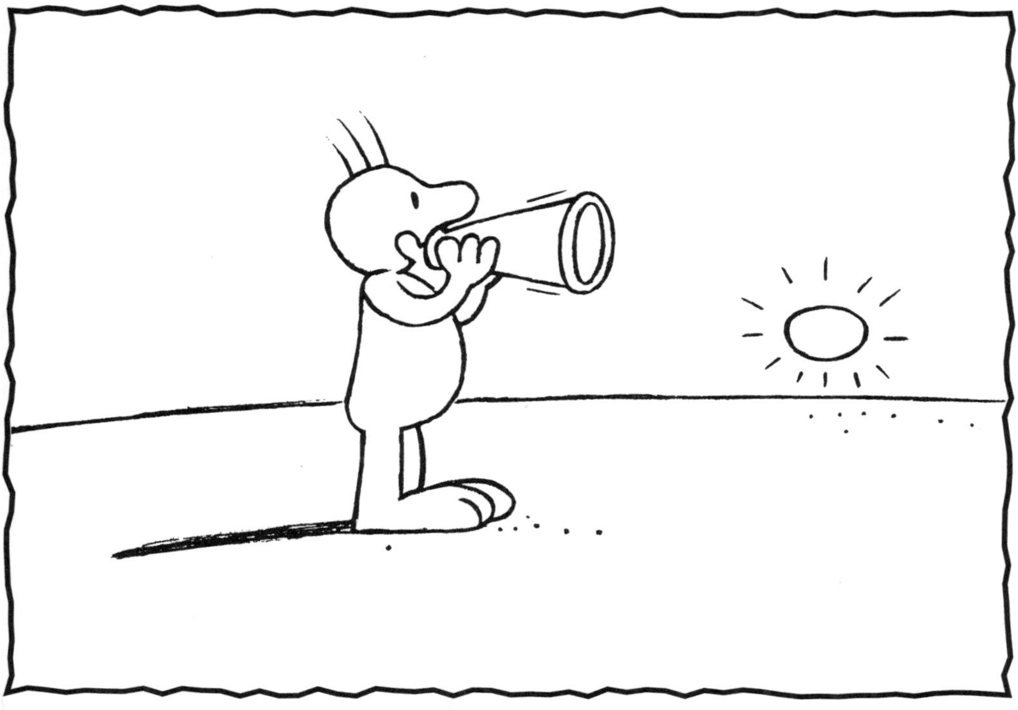

Imagination is more important
than knowledge.

Albert Einstein

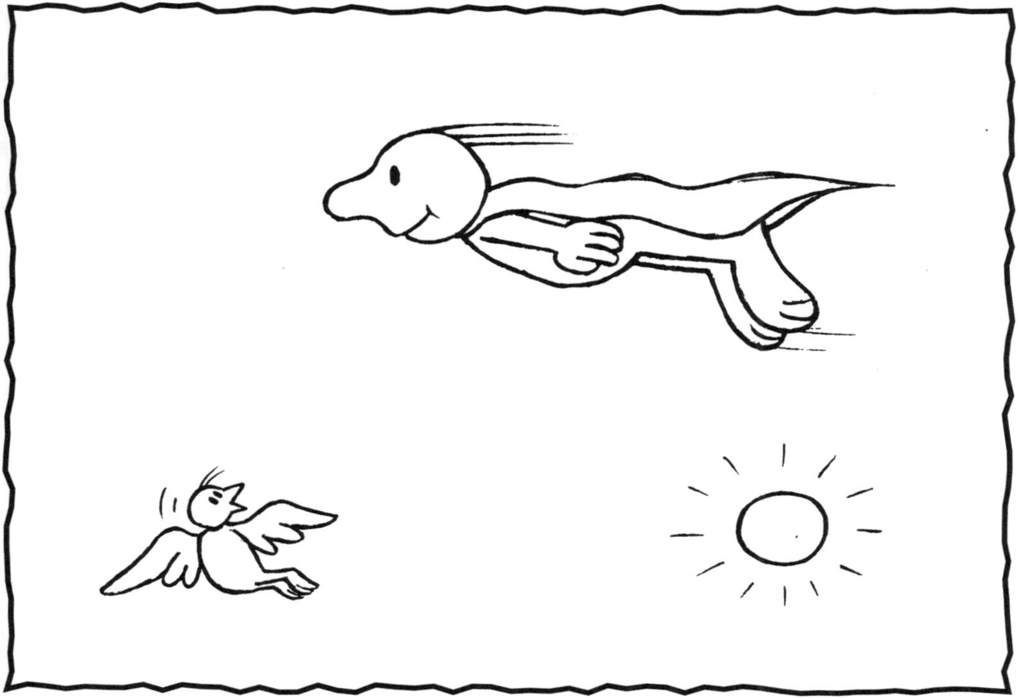

Most kids hear what you say;
some kids do what you say;
but all kids do what you do.

Kathleen Casey Theisa

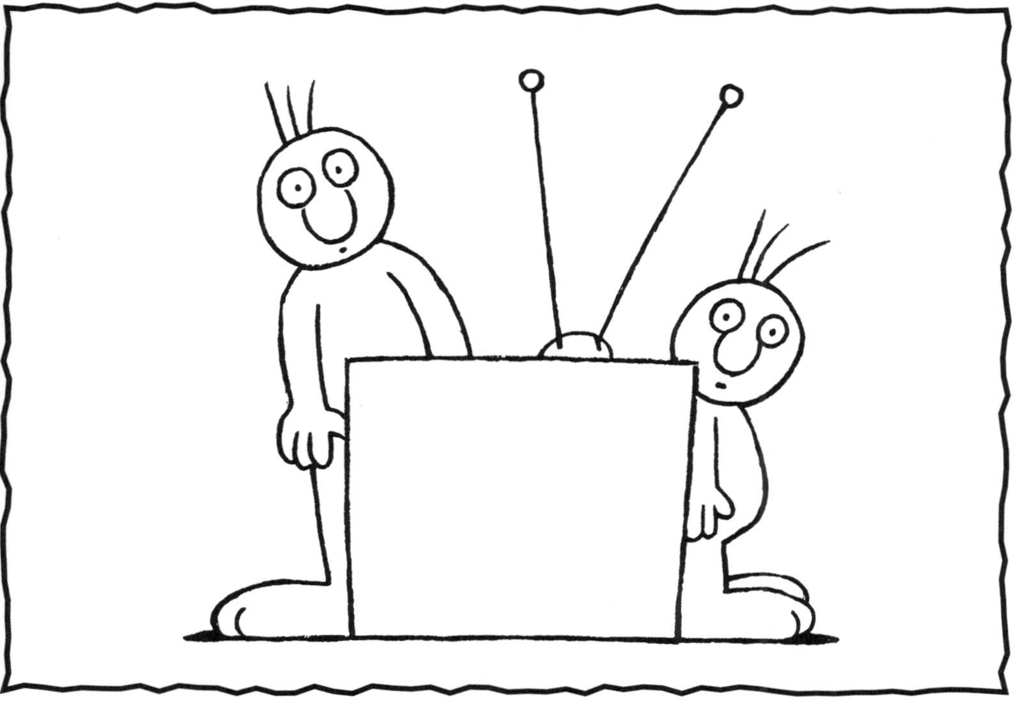

A tornado touched down, uprooting a large tree in the front yard and demolishing the house across the street. Dad went to the door, opened it, surveyed the damage, and muttered, " Darned kids..."

Tim Conway

The toughest job you'll ever love.

U. S. Army Slogan

The best thing to spend on your
children is your time.

Louise Hart

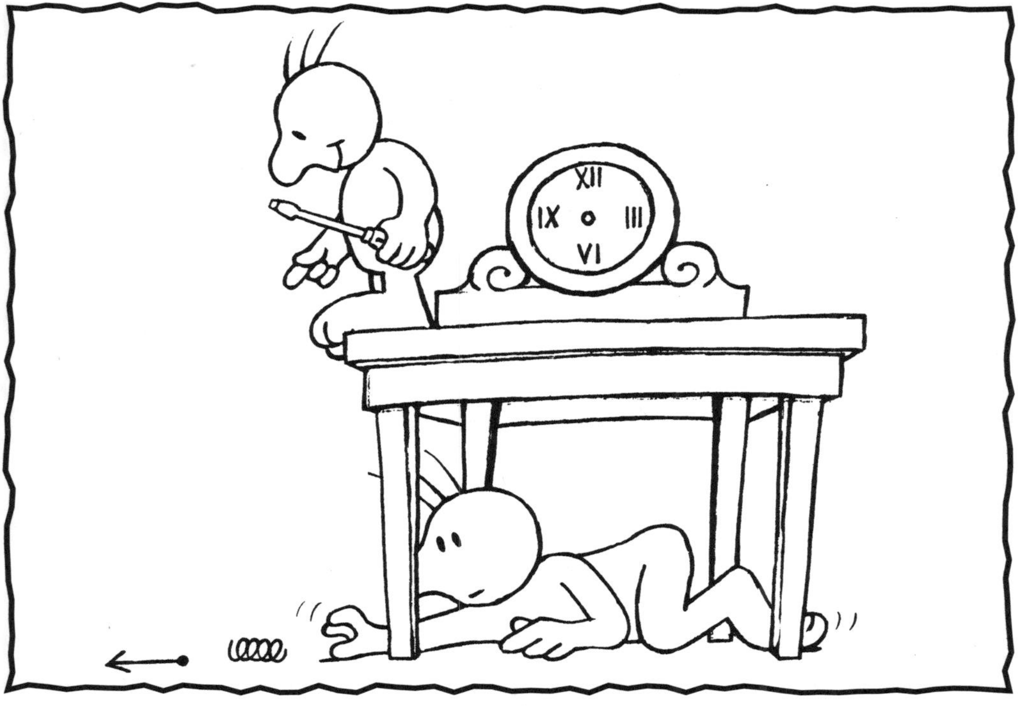
XII
IX
III
VI

Children are unpredictable.
You never know what inconsistency
they're going to catch you in next.

Franklin P. Jones

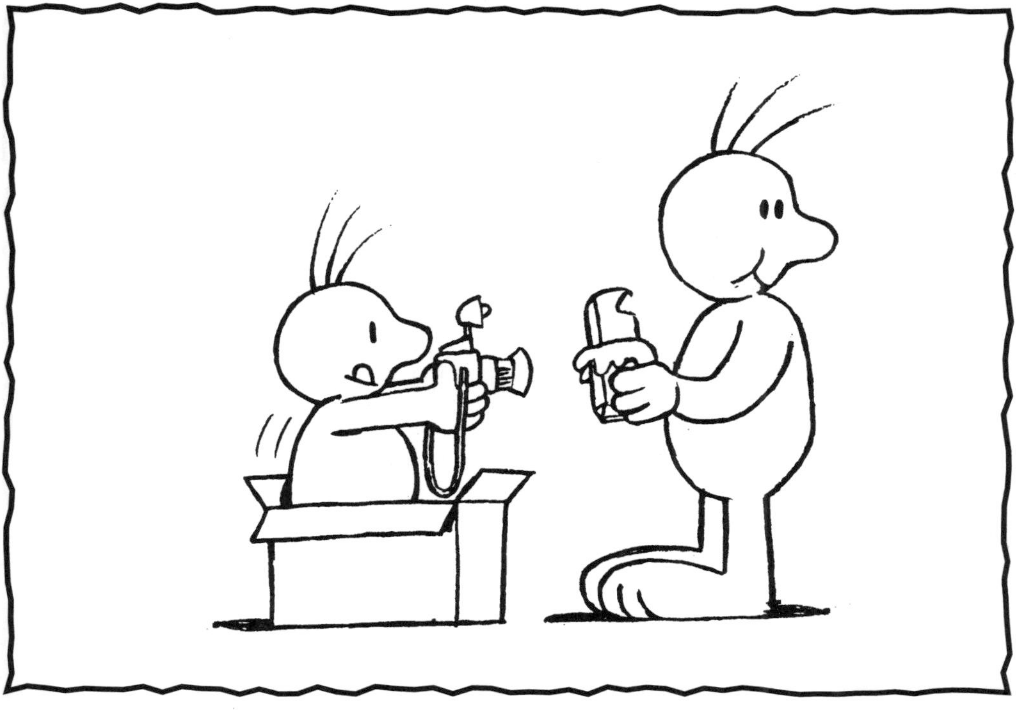

When you give your children
material things as replacements for
love, you teach them that it is
objects, not love, which will
bring them happiness.

Barbara De Angelis

Children are a great comfort in
your old age – and they help you
reach it faster too.

Lionel Kauffman.

The best security for old age is
to respect and honor your children.

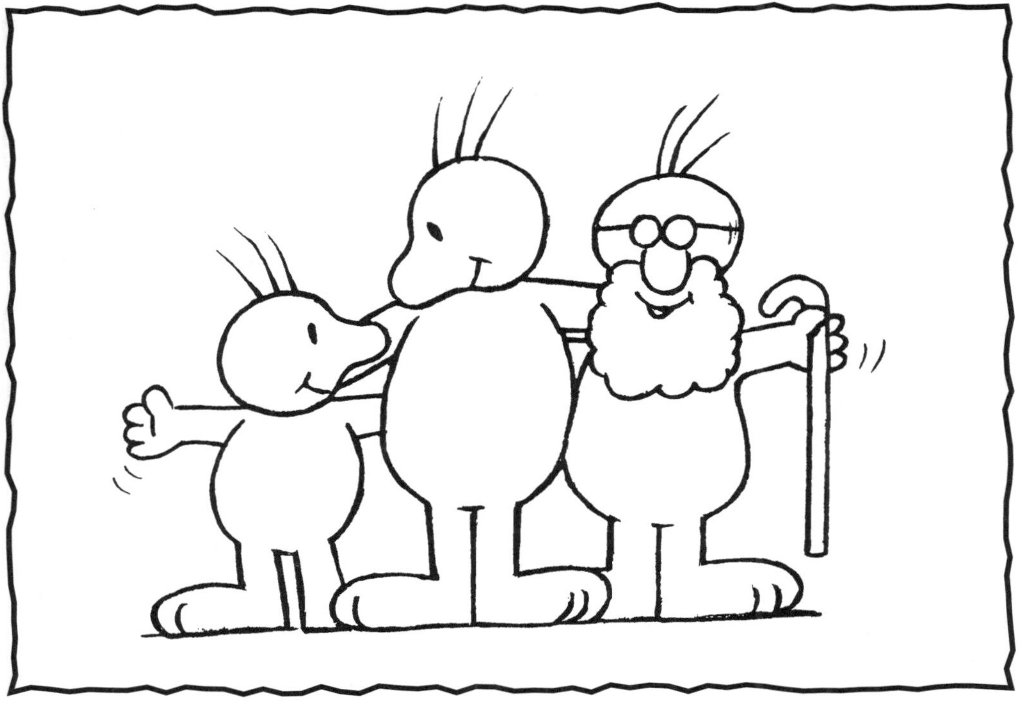

I have found the best way to give
advice to your children is
to find out what they want
and then to advise them to do it.

Harry S. Truman

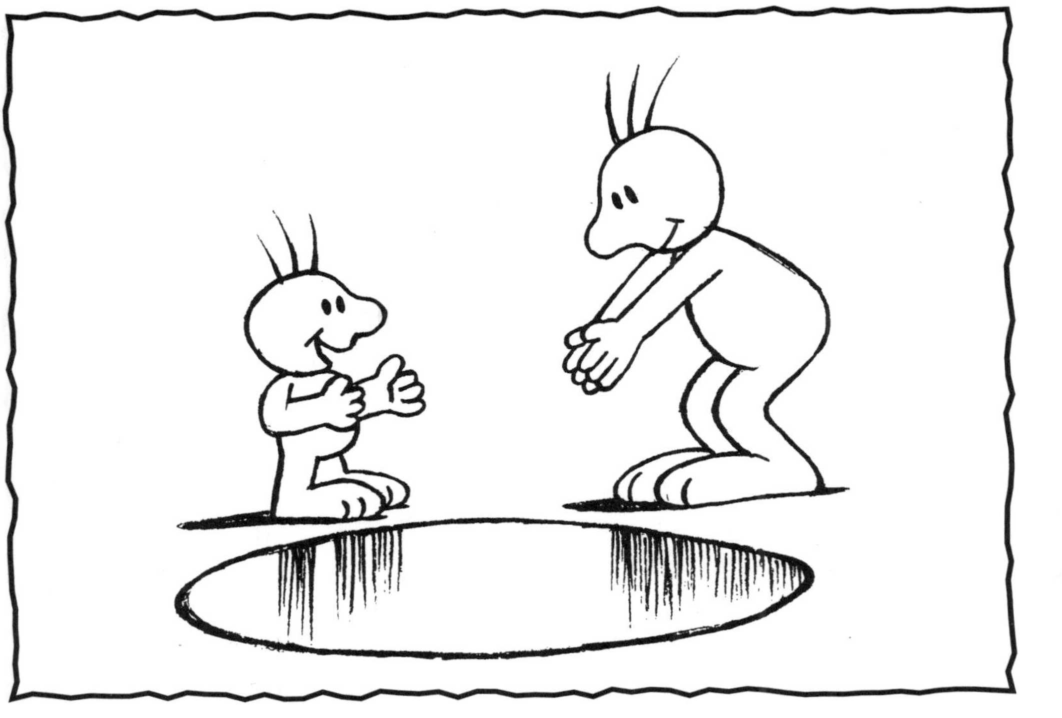

Perhaps a child who is fussed over
gets a feeling of destiny;
he thinks he is in the world for
something important
and it gives him drive and
confidance.

Dr. Benjamin Spock

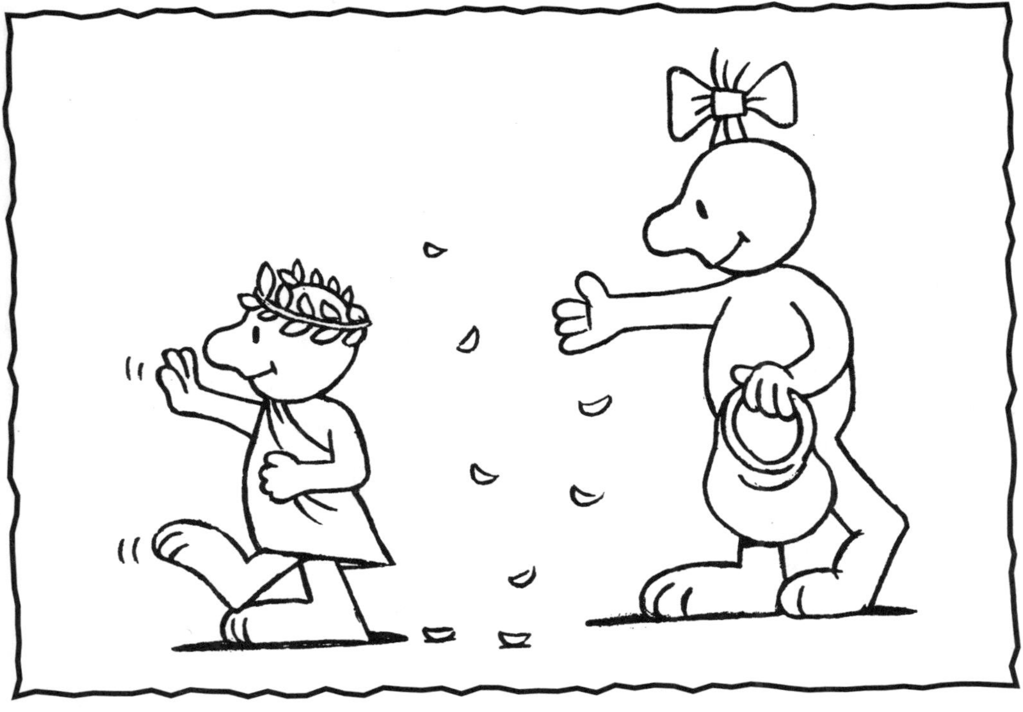

I've long since retired, my son's moved away
I called him up just the other day
I said, I'd like to see you if you don't mind
He said, I'd love to dad if I could find the time
You see, my new job's a hassle and the kids got the flu
But it's sure nice talking to you
And as I hung up the phone, it occured to me
He'd grown up just like me
My boy was just like me.

Harry Chapin

78

To become a father is not hard,
to be a father is, however.

Wilhelm Busch

Could I climb to the highest place in Athens,
I would lift my voice and proclaim,
"Fellow citizens, why do you turn and
scrape every stone to gather wealth and
take so little care of your children to
whom one day you must relinquish it all?"

Socrates

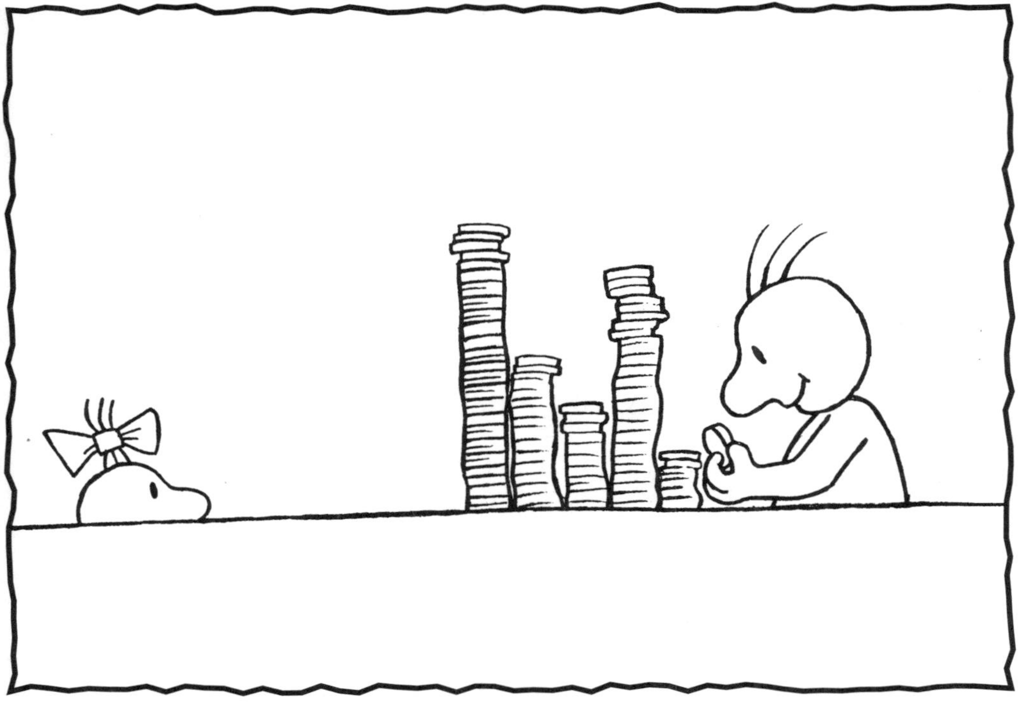

Hundreds of stars in the pretty sky,
Hundreds of shells on the shore together,
Hundreds of birds that go singing by,
Hundreds of birds in the sunny weather.

Hundreds of dewdrops to greet the dawn,
Hundreds of bees in the purple clover,
Hundreds of butterflies on the lawn,
But only one mother the wide world over.

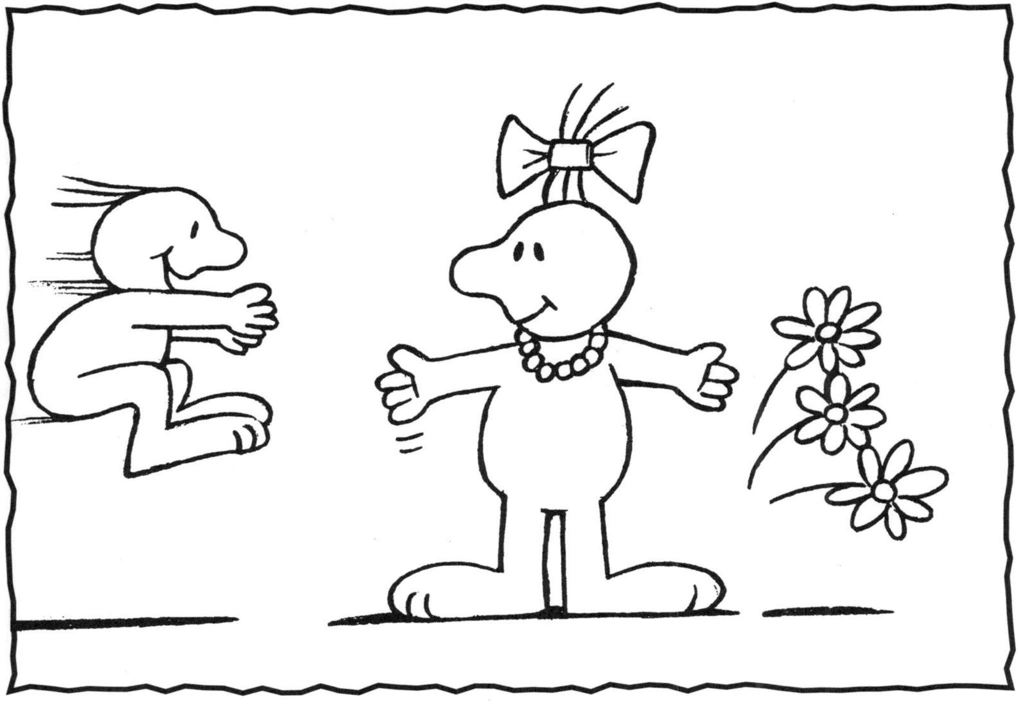

You feel so much love for your first
child that you wonder how you
could possibly love the second one
as much. Then you discover how
infinite your capacity to love is.

Linda D'Agrosa

84

Making the decision to have a child
– It's wondrous. It is to decide
forever to have your heart go
walking around outside your body.

Elizabeth Stone

All children wear the sign: "I want to be important now." Many of our juvenile delinquency problems arise because nobody bothers to read the sign.

Dan Pursuit

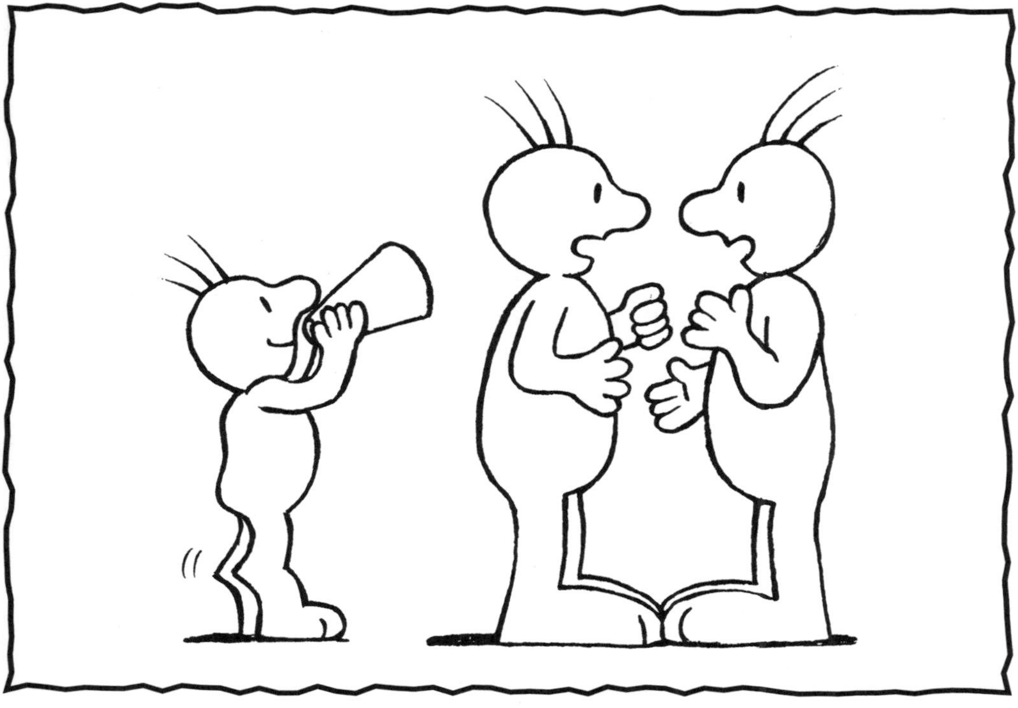

Do you know what you are?
You are unique.
In all the world, there is no
child exactly like you.

Pablo Casals

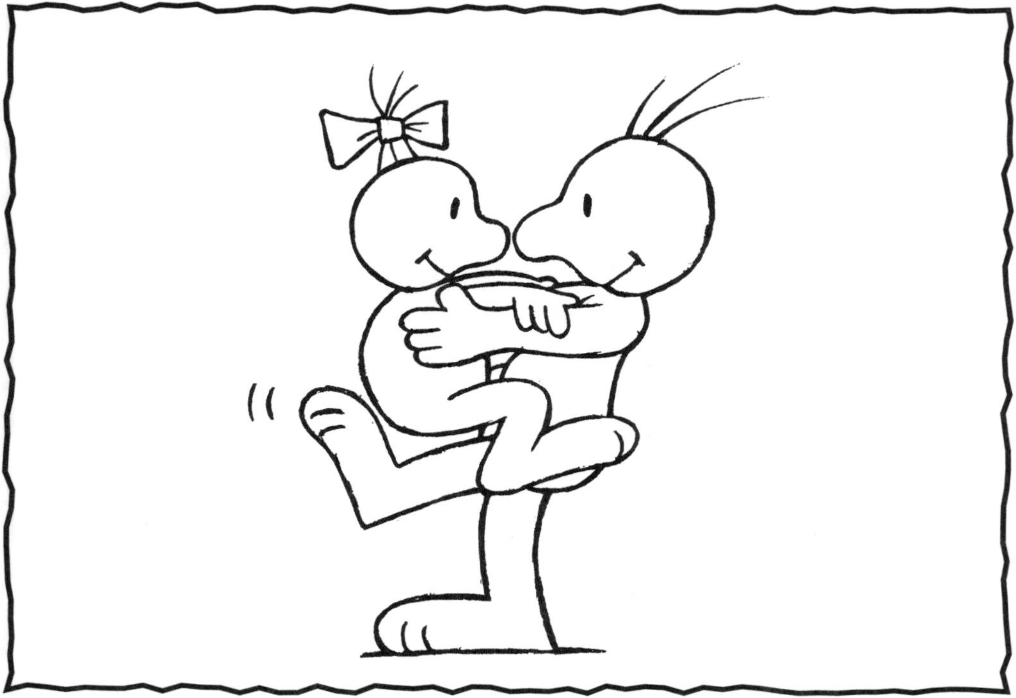

Children are not lovable for
what they do.
Children are lovable just
because they are.

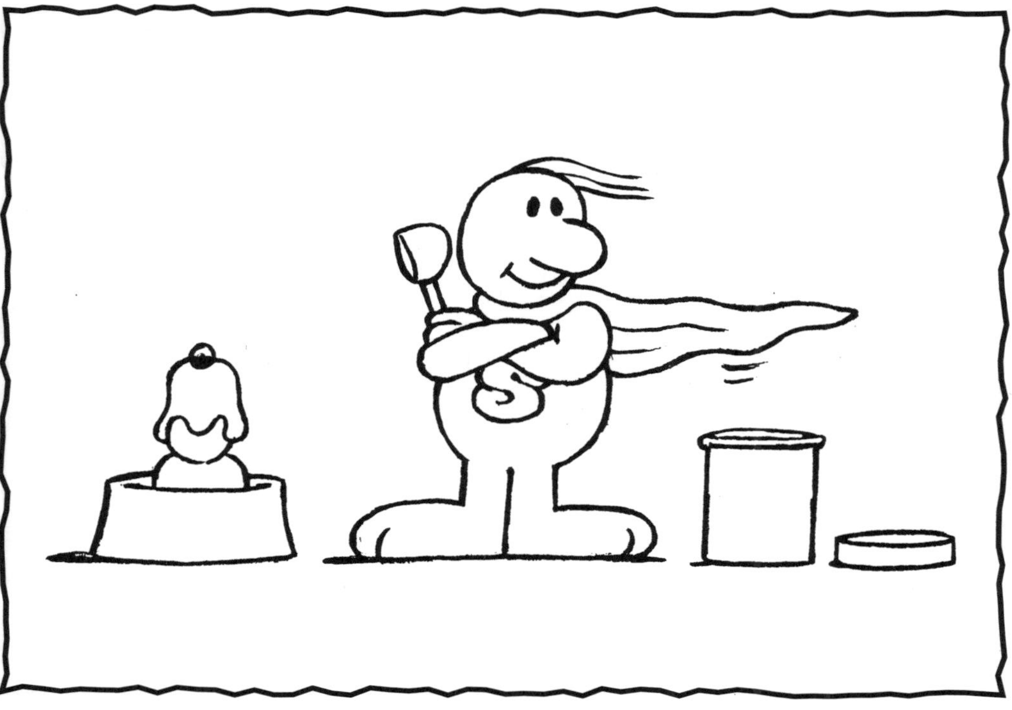

It's time for every one of us to roll up
our sleeves and get to work to save
our children. Let's stop blaming
others for children's problems and
pretending that someone else is
responsible for fixing them.
Assign yourself!

Marian Wright Edelman

Many things we need can wait.
The child cannot.
Now is the time
his bones are being formed;
his blood is being made;
his mind is being developed.
To him we cannot say tomorrow.
His name is today.

Gabriella Mistral

Reading opens up
new worlds to children.

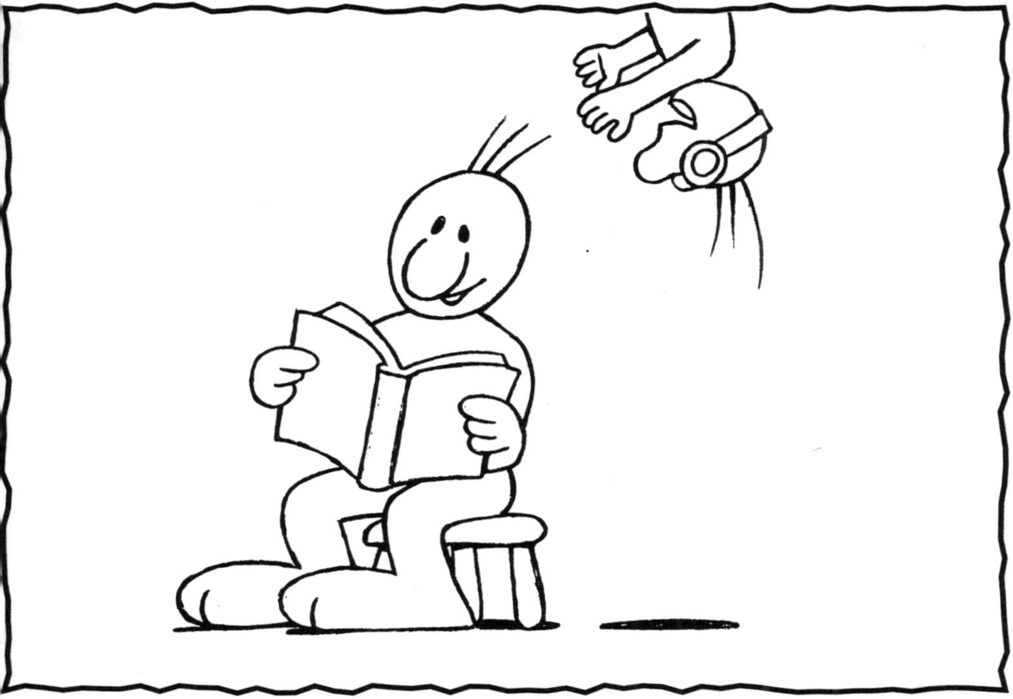

Children are meant to
be seen and heard
(and cherished and honored
and loved lots and lots).

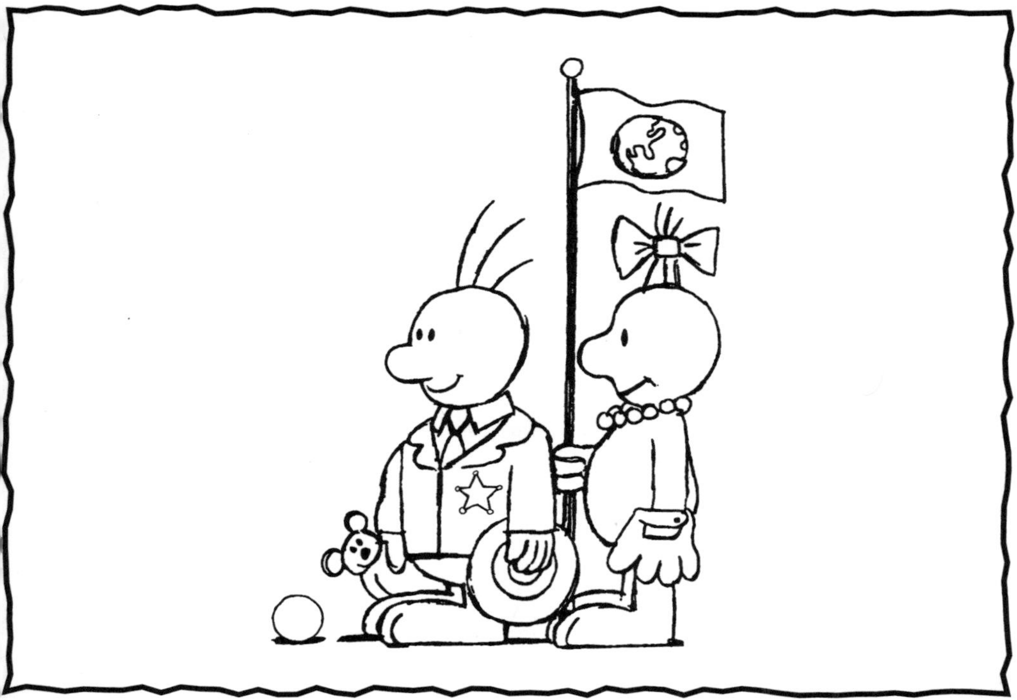

That energy which makes a child hard to
manage is the energy which afterward
makes him a manager of life.

Henry Ward Beecher

The time and the quality of the time
that their parents devote to them
indicate to children the degree to which
they are valued by their parents...
When children know that they are
valued, when they truly feel valued in
the deepest part of themselves, then
they feel valuable. This knowledge is
worth more than gold.

M. Scott Peck

Support wildlife.
Throw a party.

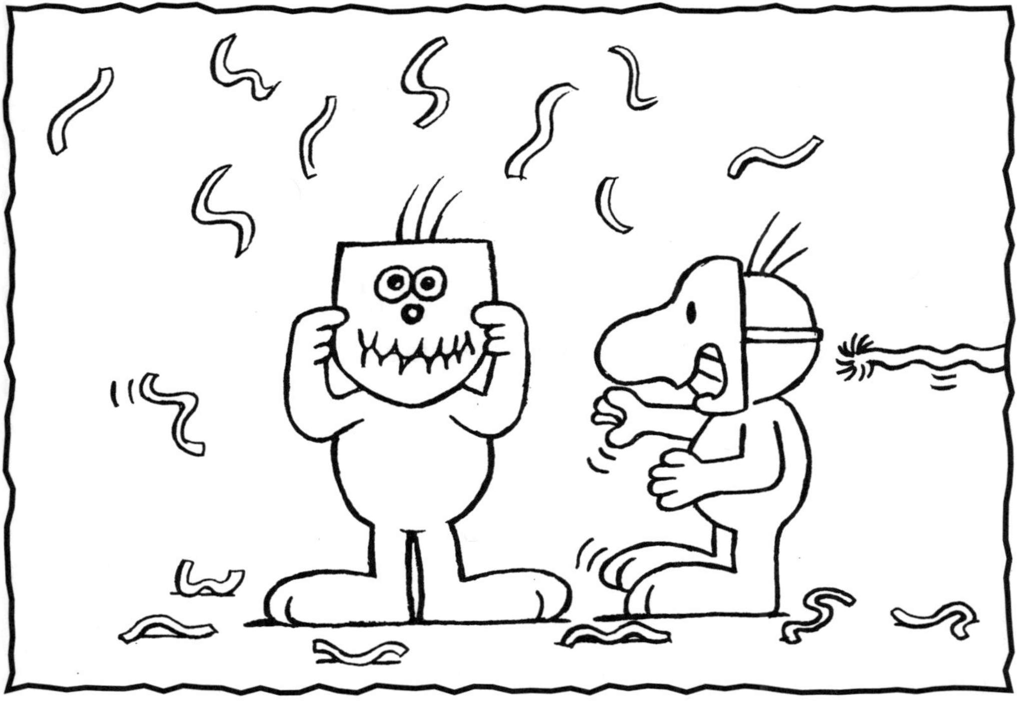

Children can because we help them
to believe in themselves.

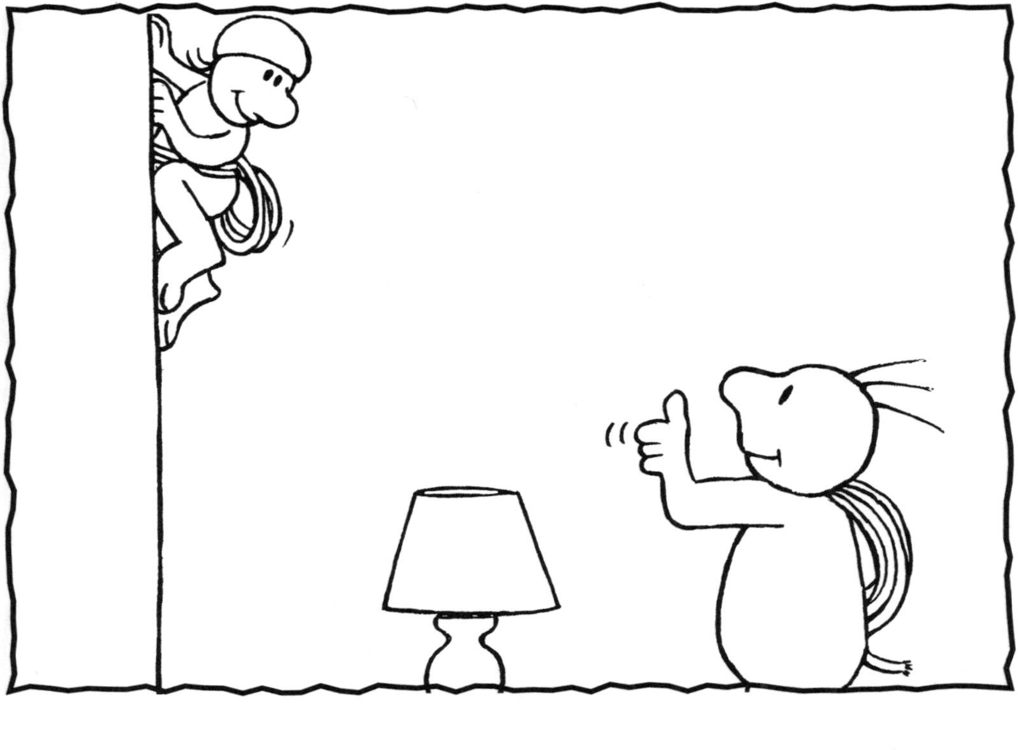

Attitudes are caught, not taught.

Quaker saying

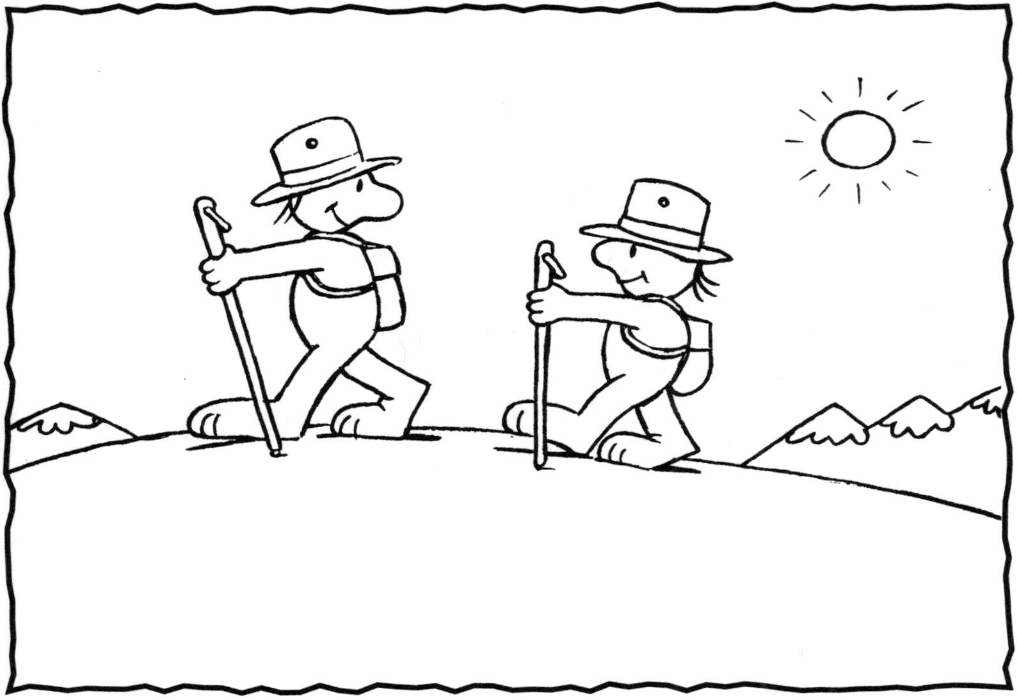

When God wants an important thing done in this world or a wrong righted, He goes about it in a very singular way. He doesn't release thunderbolts or stir up earthquakes. God simply has a tiny baby born, perhaps of a very humble home, perhaps of a very humble mother. And God puts the idea or purpose into the mother's heart. And she puts it in the baby's mind, and then — God waits. The great events of this world are not battles and elections and earthquakes and thunderbolts. The great events are babies, for each child comes with the message that God is not yet discouraged with humanity, but is still expecting goodwill to become incarnate in each human life.

Edmond McDonald

106

You give but little when you give
of your possessions.
It is when you give of yourself
that you truly give.

Kahlil Gibran

Example is not the main thing
in influencing others.
It is the only thing.

Albert Schweitzer

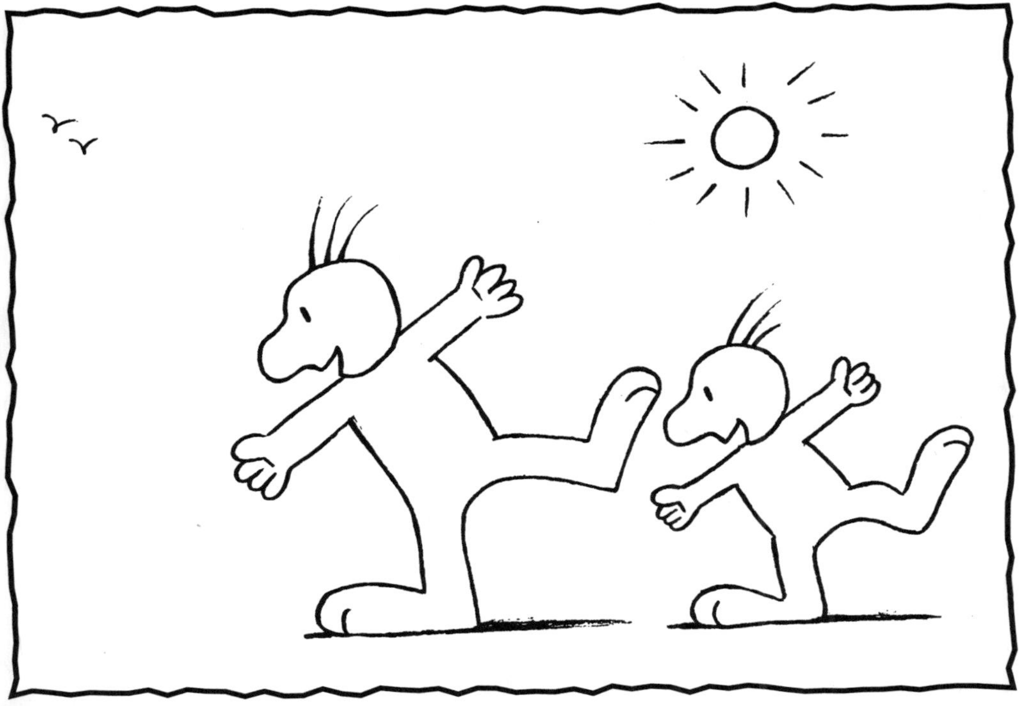

Children don't ask for things
they don't want.
They just don't want them
after they get them.

Howard Stevens

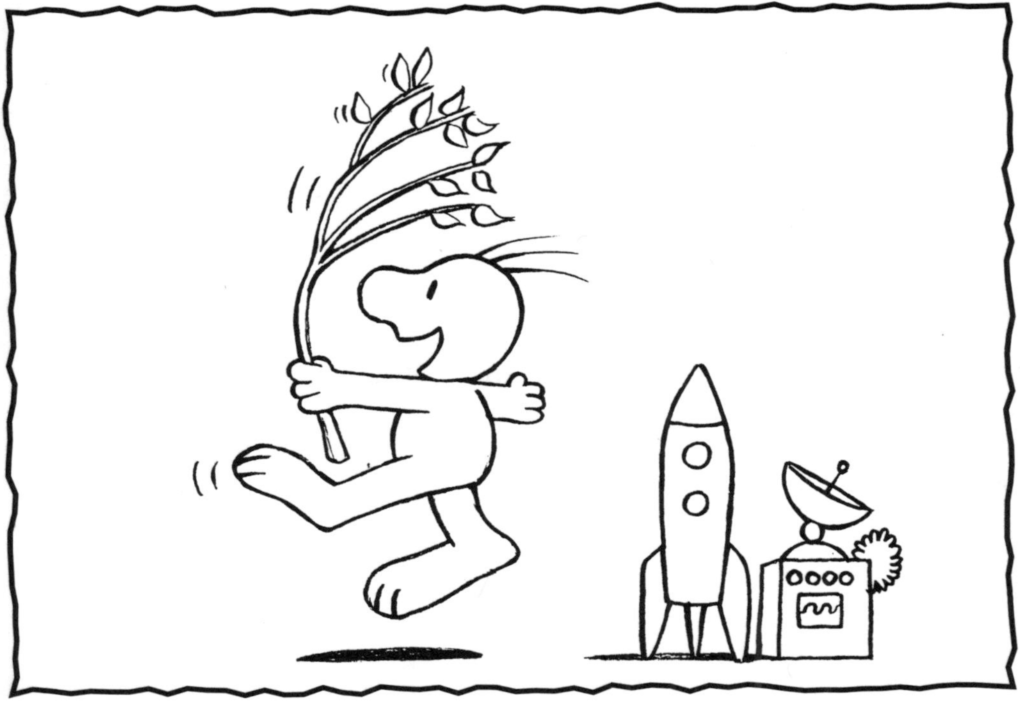

The elders still stay:
"You know I have been young once,
but you never have been old."
But todays kids can reply:
"You've never been young in
the world I am young in,
and you never can be."

Margaret Mead

Parenthood remains the greatest
single preserve of the amateur.

Alvin Toffler

Every time a baby's existence... is celebrated, a tiny piece is added to the foundation of that baby's future self-image, self confidence and social competence.

Penelope Leach

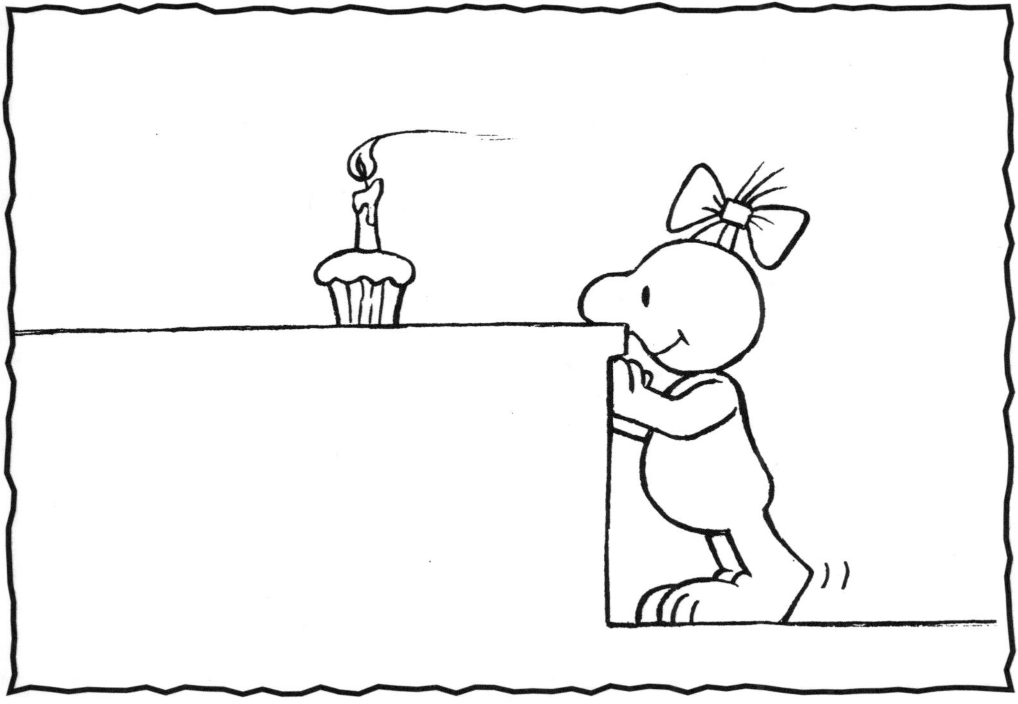

What children really need is love.

Jeff Kahn

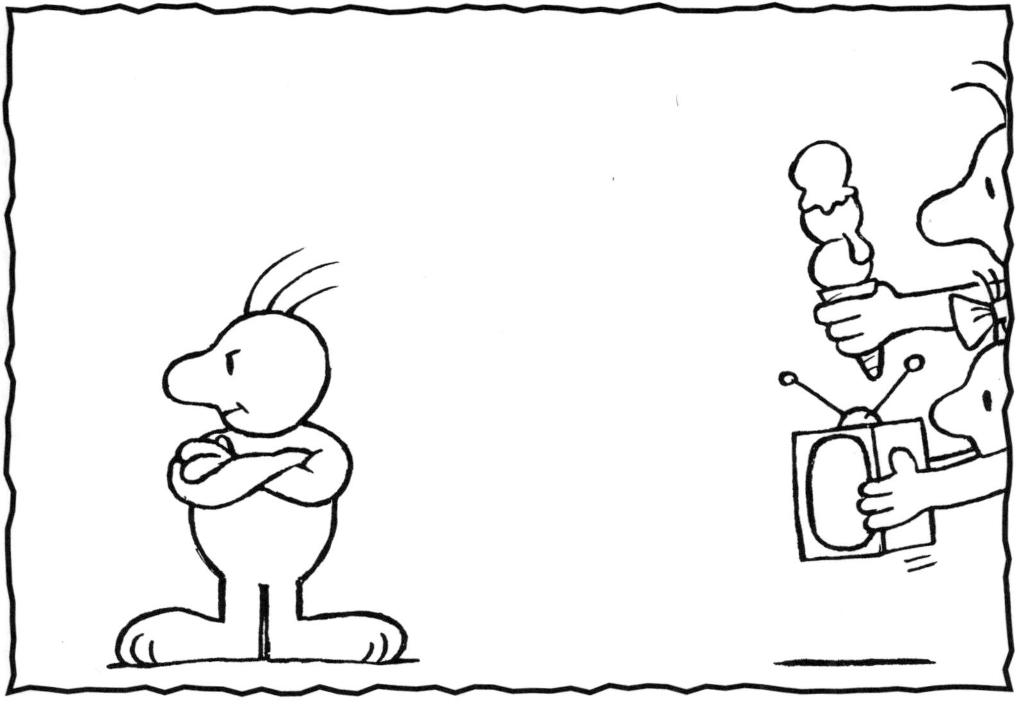

There are times when parenthood
seems nothing but feeding the
mouth that bites you.

Peter De Vries

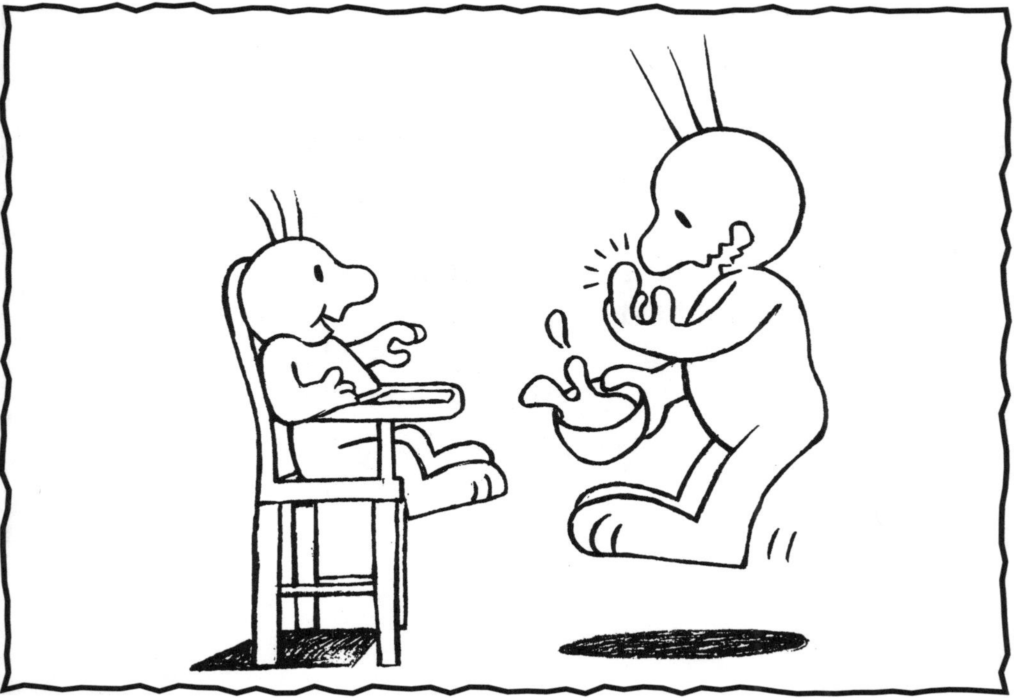

She broke the bread into two fragments and gave them to the children, who ate with avidity. "She hath kept none for herself," grumbled the Sergeant. "Because she is not hungry," said a soldier. "Because she is a mother," said the Sergeant.

Victor Hugo

At work, you think of the children
you have left at home. At home,
you think of the work you've left
unfinished. Such a struggle is
unleashed within yourself.
Your heart is rent.

Golda Meir

At every step the child should
be allowed to meet the real
experiences of life;
the thorns should never be
plucked from the roses.

Ellen Key

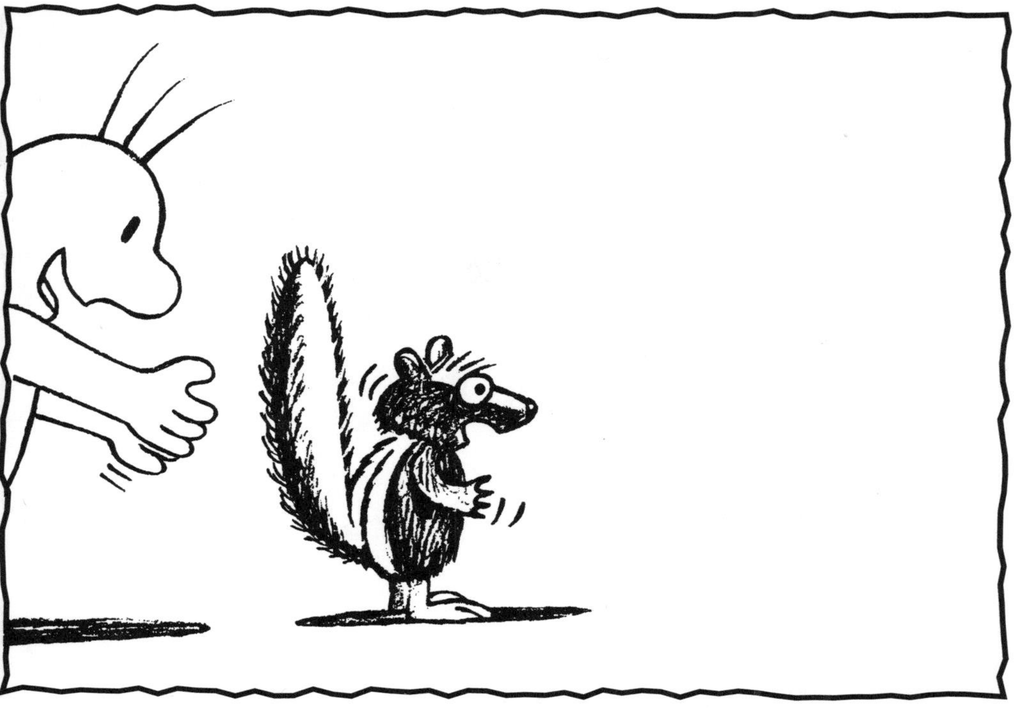

A child is the greatest
poem ever known.

Christopher Morley

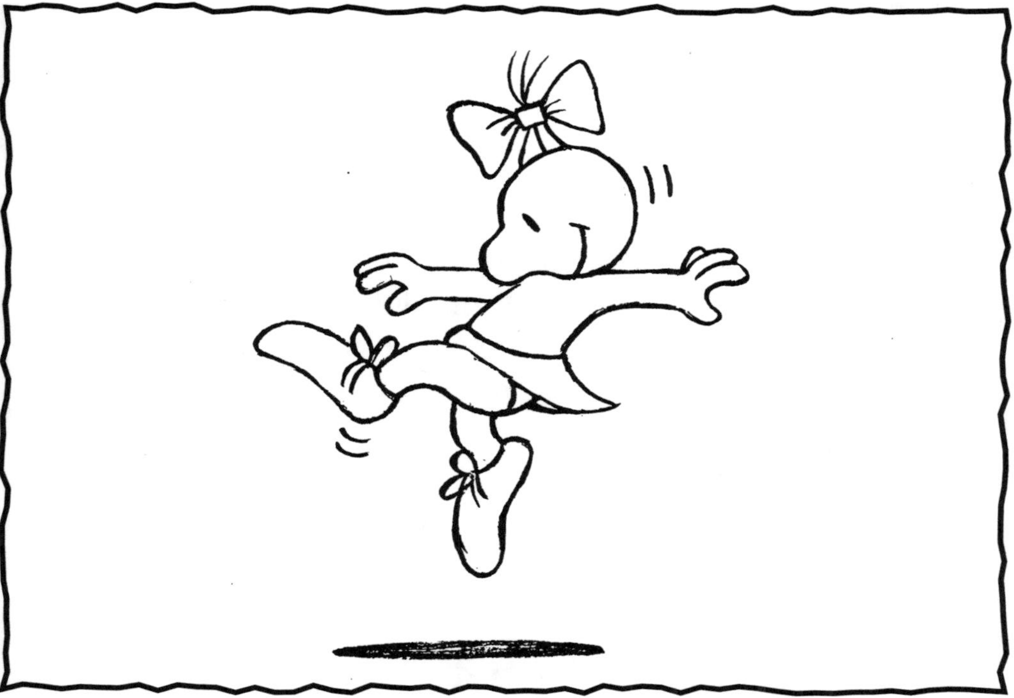

Teach your children
to brush their teeth,
brush their hair
and brush the dog,
but not with the same brush.
The dog resents it.

Peggy Goldtrap

The best way to keep children
home is to make the home a
pleasant atmosphere – and let
the air out of the tires.

Dorothy Parker

Nobody can do for little children
what grandparents do.
Grandparents sort of sprinkle
stardust over the lives of
little children.

Alex Haley

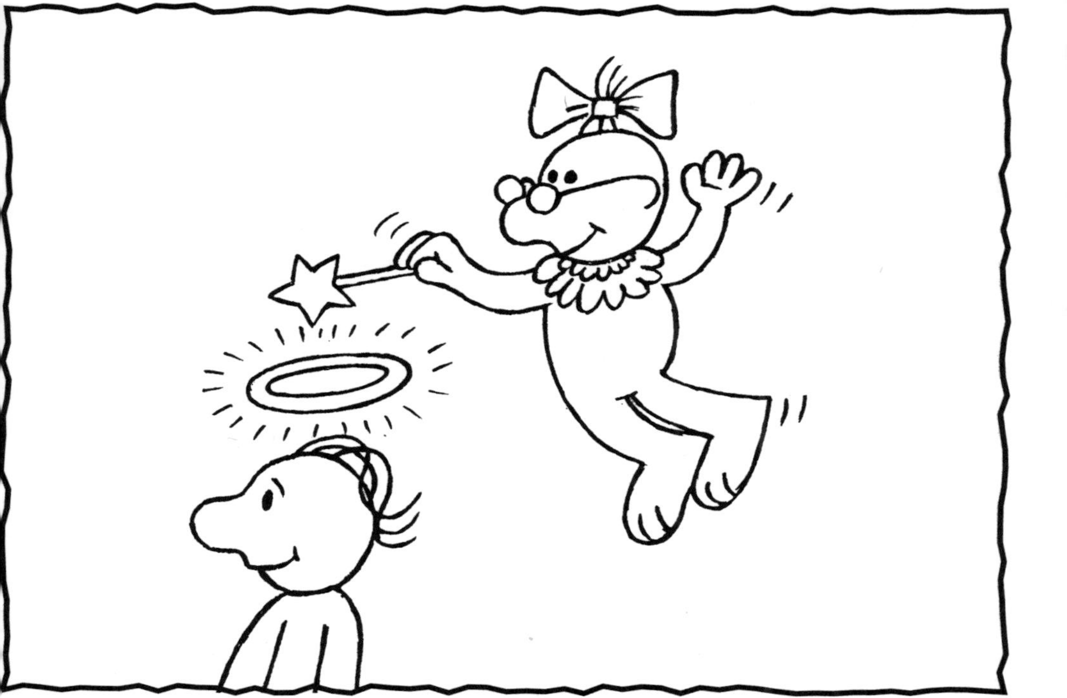

Hand over your chocolate
and nobody gets hurt.

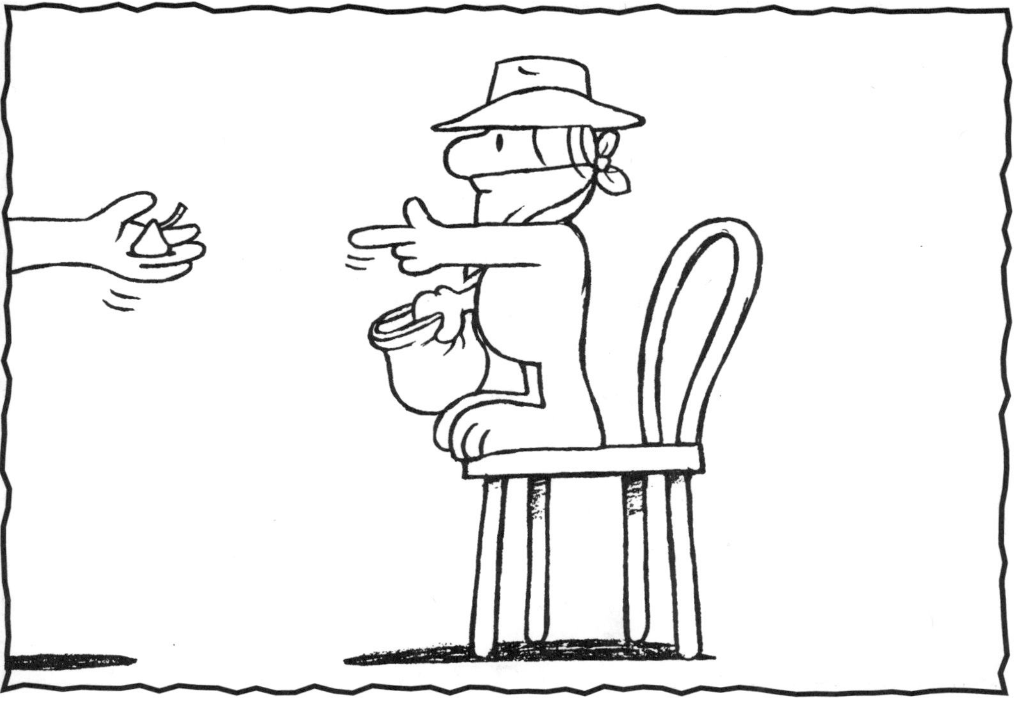

The secret of education lies in
respecting the pupil.

Ralph Waldo Emerson

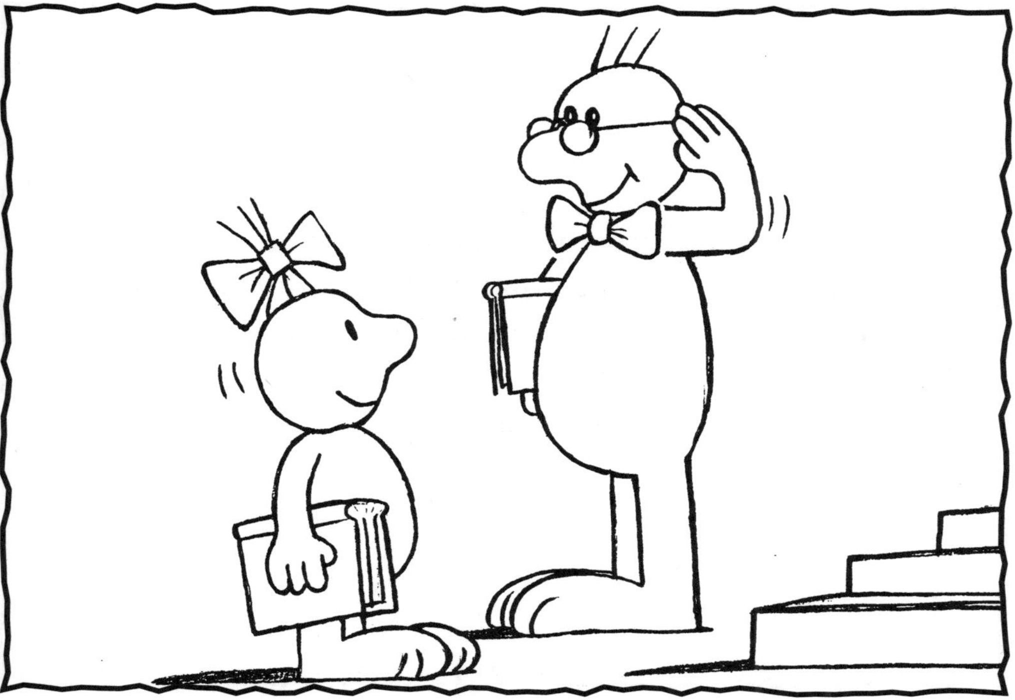

Our attitude toward the newborn child should
be one of reverence that a spiritual being has
been confined within limits perceptable to us.

Maria Montessori

Life is a flame that is
always burning itself out,
but it catches fire again
every time a child is born.

George Bernard Shaw

Happiness comes from noticing and
enjoying the little things in life.

Barbara Ann Kipfer

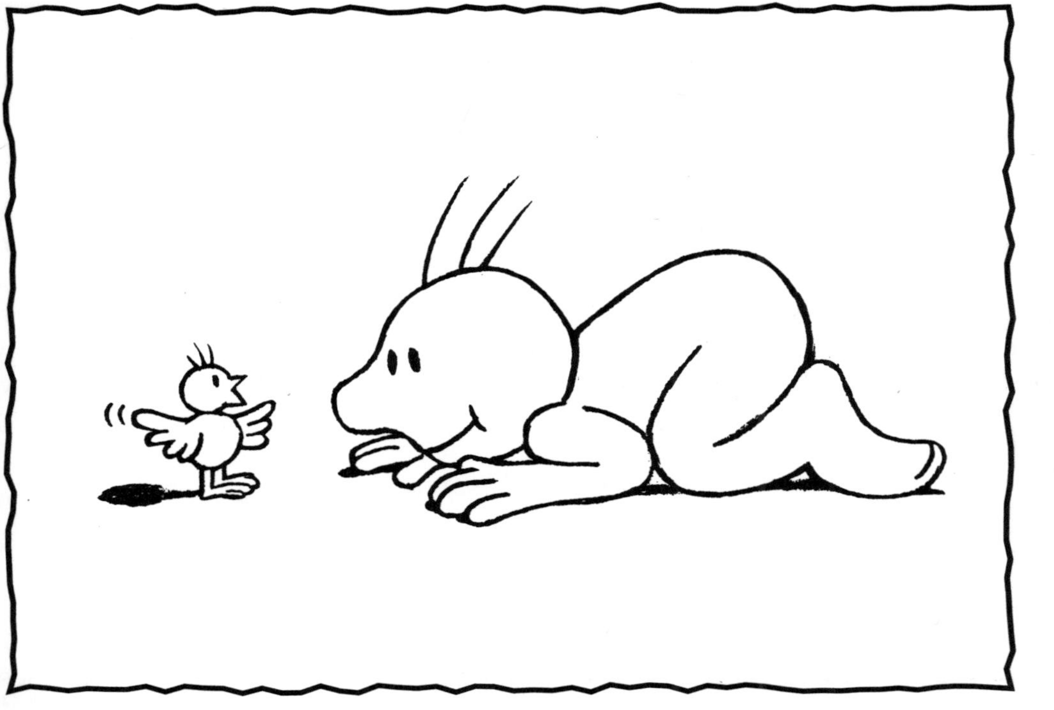

If you are violent with your children
they are more likely to be violent
with their playmates.
If you hit them as punishment for a
misdeed a child will learn that
violence is appropriate behavior.

Dr. Benjamin Spock

138

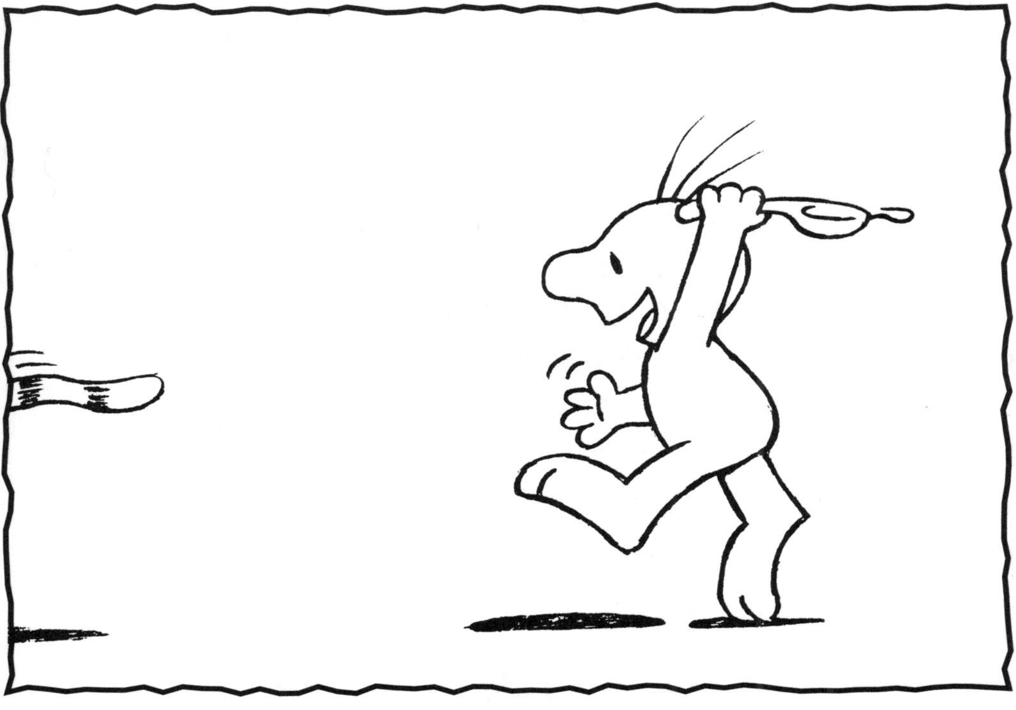

Children desperately need to know –
and to hear in ways they understand and remember –
that they're loved and valued
by Mom and Dad.

Gary Smalley and Paul Trent

Strengthen a parent...
and you strengthen a child.

Fred Rogers

We find delight in the beauty and
happiness of children that makes
the heart too big for the body.

Ralph Waldo Emerson

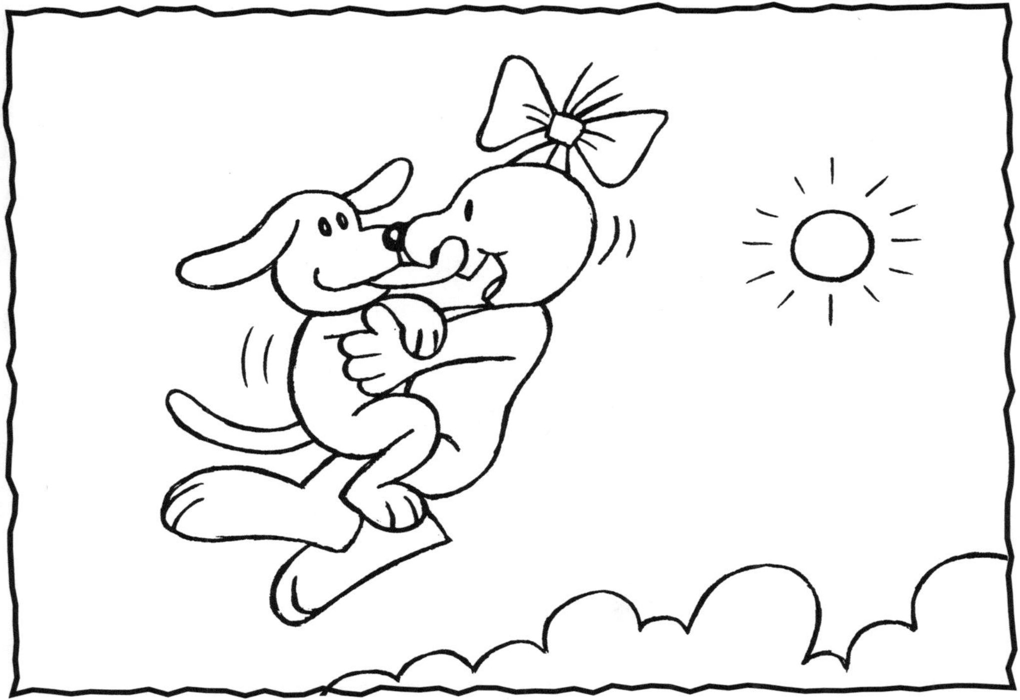

The applause of a single human being
is of great consequence.

James Boswell

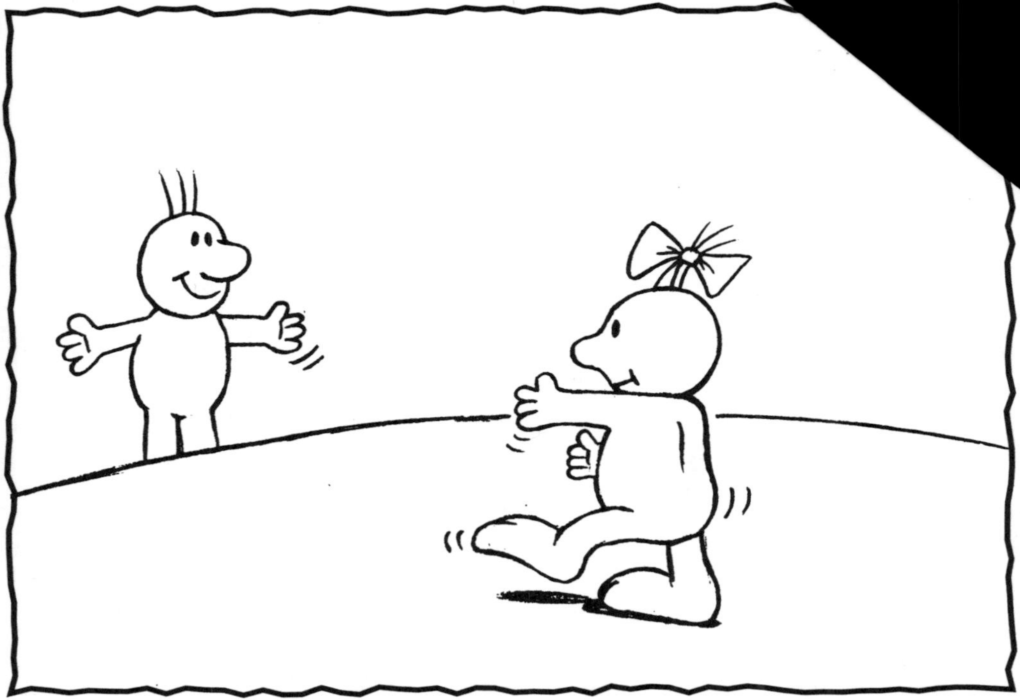

. your forgiveness for all the times I
ked when I should have listened;
gry when I should have been patient;
acted when I should have waited;
feared when I should have been delighted;
scolded when I should have encouraged;
criticized when I should have complimented;
said no when I should have said yes and
said yes when I should have said no.

Marian Wright Edelman

146

Raising children is a creative endeavor,
an art, rather than a science.

Bruno Bettelheim

There is no more vital calling or
vocation for men than fathering.

John R. Troop

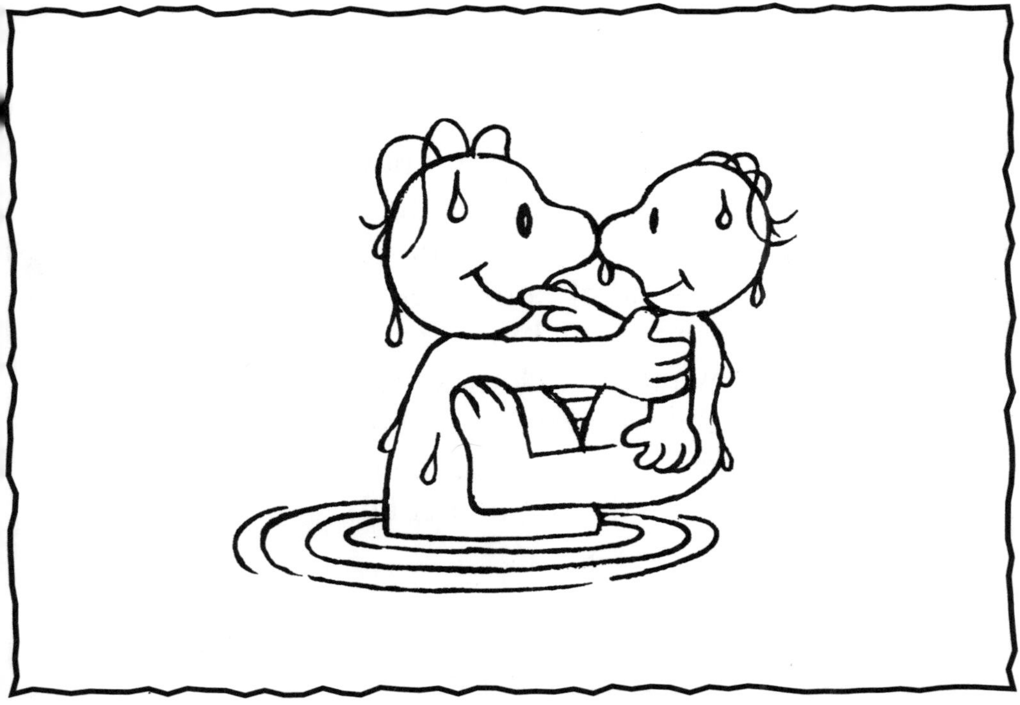

Fifty years from now,
it will not matter
what kind of car you drove,
what kind of house you lived in,
how much you had in your bank account
nor what your clothes looked like.
But the world will be a little better
because you were important
in the life of a child.

150

Children are the most
valuable natural resource.

Herbert Hoover

Keeping a house clean
with young children
is like shoveling the walk
before it stops snowing.

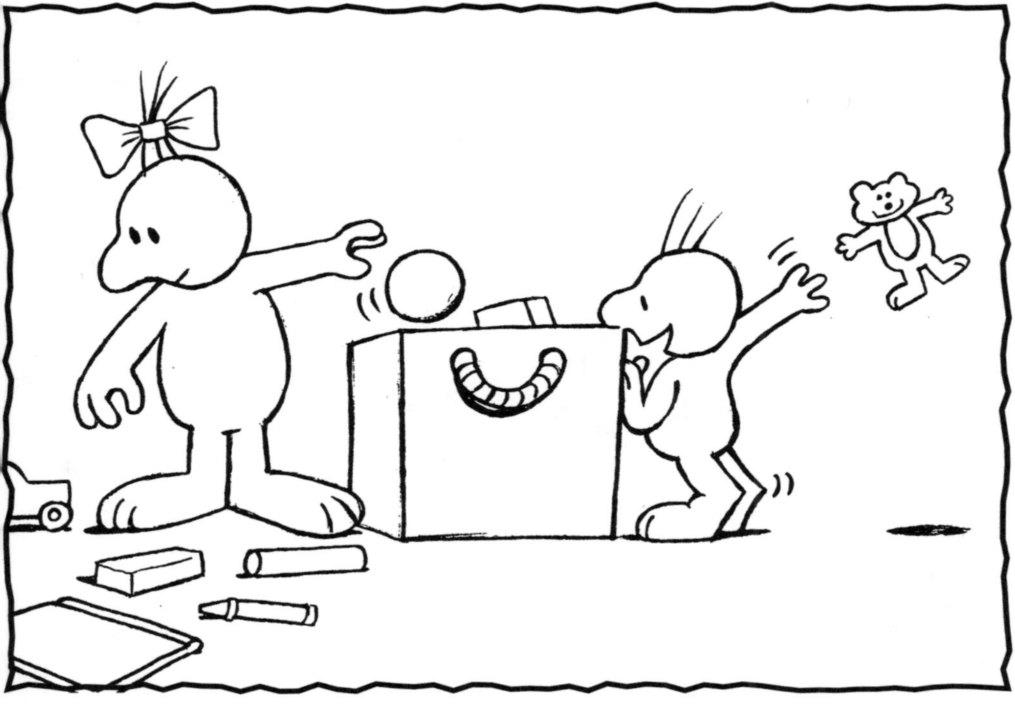

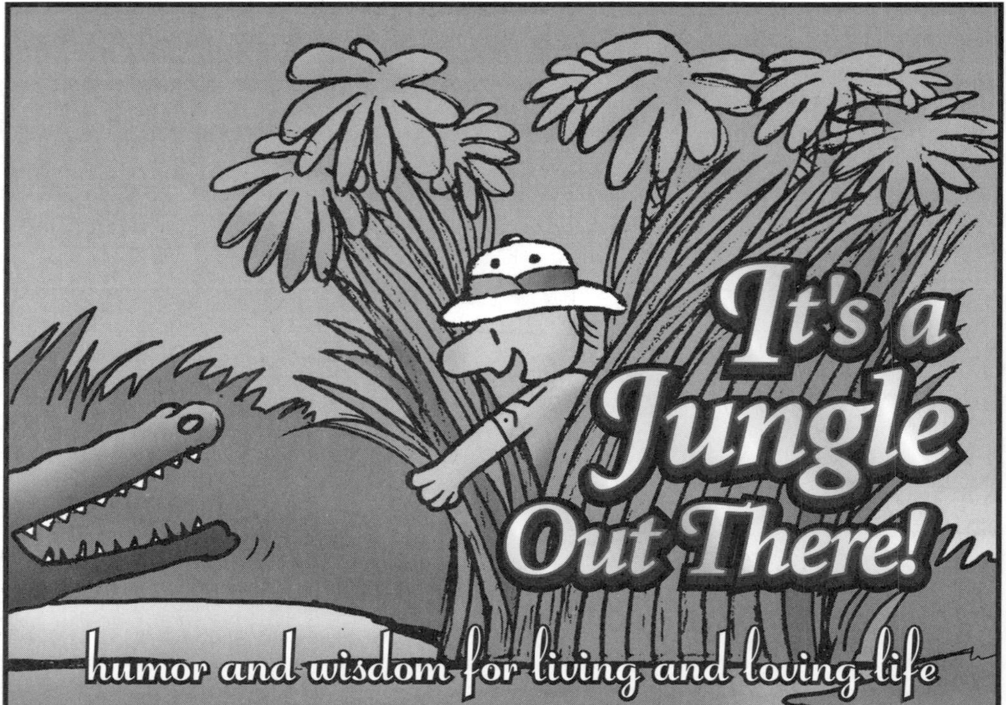
It's a Jungle Out There!
humor and wisdom for living and loving life

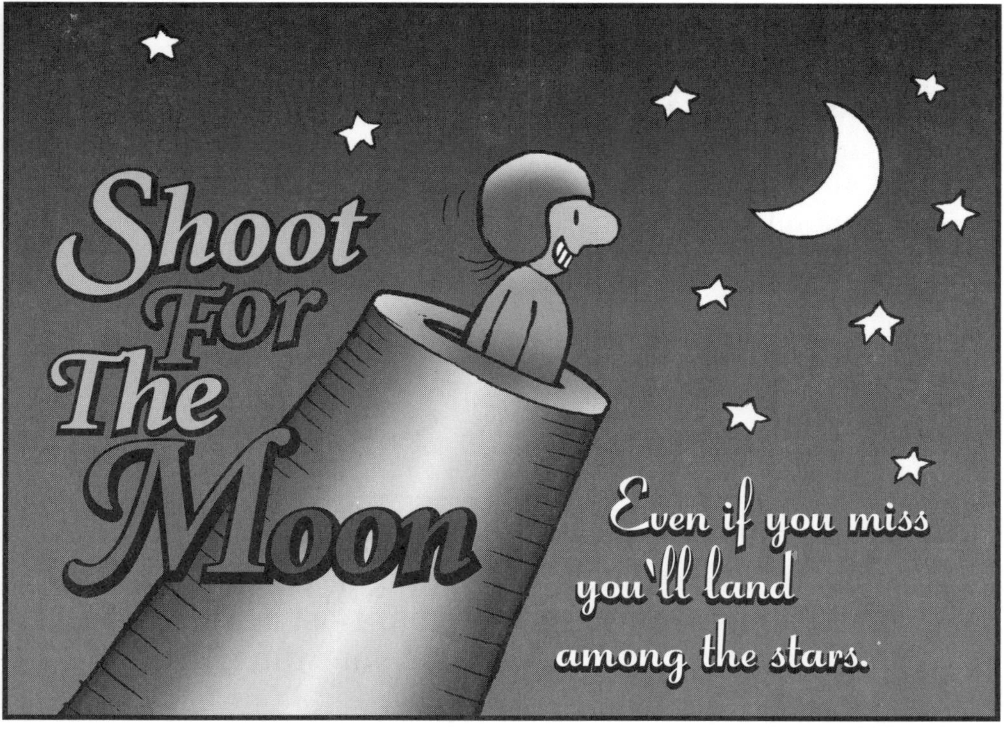
Shoot For The Moon
Even if you miss you'll land among the stars.

Relax, God is in Charge

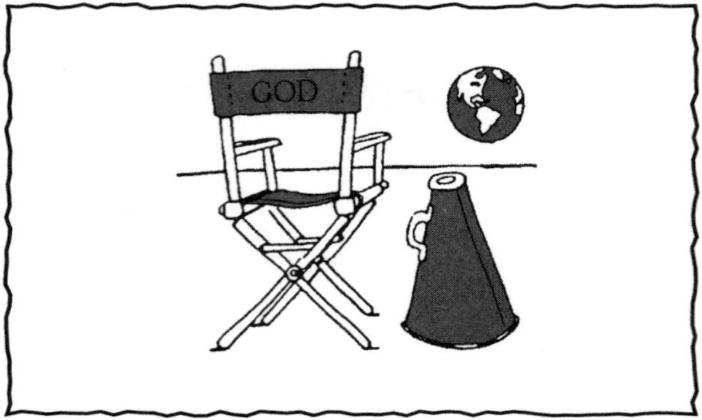
GOD

and 77 other inspirational illustrations and thoughts to enable you to go right, disable you from going wrong, stick to your ribs, warm the cockles of your heart and tickle your funny bone.

When Life Gives You Lemons...

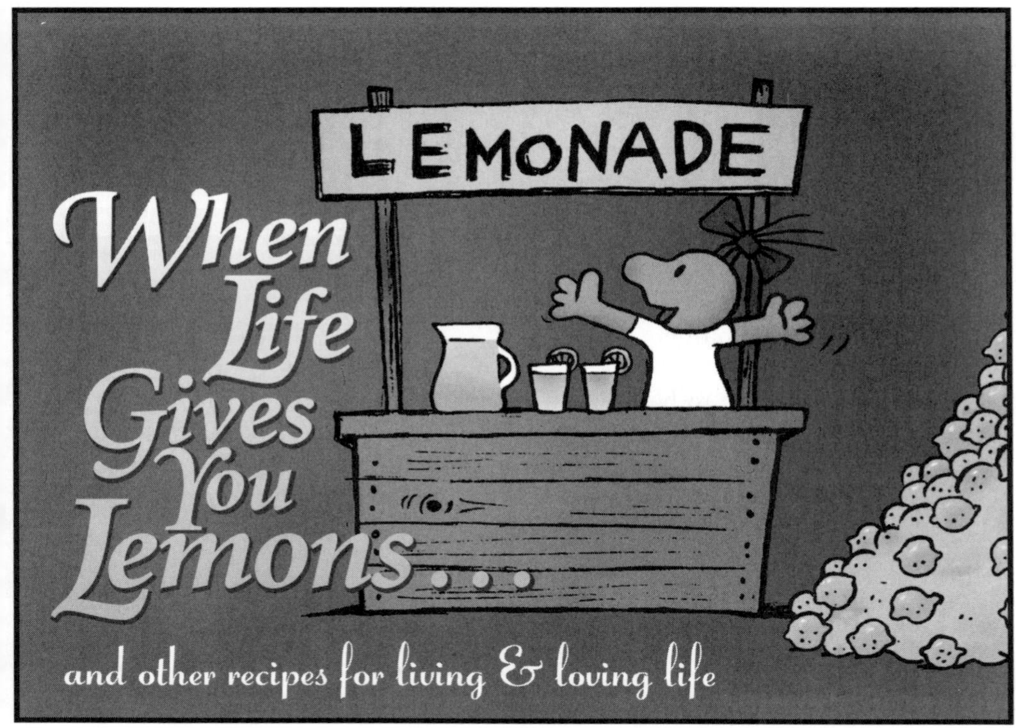
LEMONADE

and other recipes for living & loving life

P.O. Box 1204, Del Mar, California 92014
1-800-522-3383   Fax 619-452-2797

PuddleDancer titles available from your favorite bookstore:

Relax, God is in Charge	ISBN 0-9647349-0-7
Keep Coming Back	ISBN 0-9647349-1-5
Children are Meant to be Seen and Heard	ISBN 0-9647349-2-3
Shoot for the Moon	ISBN 0-9647349-3-1
When Life Gives You Lemons...	ISBN 0-9647349-4-X
It's a Jungle Out There!	ISBN 0-9647349-5-8

Acknowledgements

Every effort has been made to find the copyright owner of the material used.
However, there are a few quotations that have been impossible to trace, and
we would be glad to hear from the copyright owners of these quotations, so
that acknowledgement can be recognized in any future edition.